Same Cross
New Questions

How Jesus brings connection in a world
of loneliness and separation

André Adefope

malcolm down
PUBLISHING

First published 2018 by Malcolm Down Publishing Ltd.
www.malcolmdown.co.uk

British Library Cataloguing in Publication Data
A catalogue record for this book is available from the British Library.

ISBN 978-1-910786-46-8

Cover design by Esther Kotecha
Art direction by Sarah Grace

Printed and bound in Great Britain by Bell & Bain Ltd, Glasgow

Dedication

Thank you to all of my friends and family,
especially my wife, Becca, who gave me support,
read drafts of this book and gave feedback and
encouragement. You're all amazing.

What others are saying...

André hasn't just learned theology, he lives it. This is evident in this book which doesn't just communicate ideas, but communicates his heart and passion to connect us with Jesus in a way that can characterise our day-to-day living.

Ian Henderson
Founder and CEO of Visible Ministries and the Naked Truth Project

This book is a clear exploration of such an important topic: the cross. With sharp theology and clear examples, I can't more highly recommend this book.

Rev. Cris Rogers
Vicar of All Hallows Bow, and Leader of wearemakingdisciples.com

It is a great pleasure to recommend André's short and punchy book. How can the cross be important to so-called 'millennials'? André's approach is highly personal and innovative, with a lot of dialogue and narrative. It is also firmly biblical and explains his topic with clarity and energy. A very useful and relevant book – it will prove valuable to Christian leaders of all ages.

Rev. Robert Willoughby
Church Leader and former tutor at London School of Theology

A lively exploration of the riches of the cross, from one of the UK's brightest young Christian writers.

Mike Starkey
Writer, broadcaster, and creator of the Faith Pictures course

André's passion for people to know the beauty, truth and power of the gospel in all its fullness shines through in this clever and creative little book. As we make the effort to understand the richness of the Good News so that we may share it with clarity, we can be thankful to André for reminding us that the connection points from the cross of Christ are sufficient to reach any person, as we listen to the genuine concerns of their lives and share the gospel with them accordingly.

Ben Jack
Advance, The Message Evangelists Movement

Love the way that André unpacks the timeless and life-changing message of the cross, asking real questions through everyday conversation that will help people, especially those younger in faith and age, to reconnect to their loving Father God.

Sim Dendy
Senior Leader at Freedom Church UK

This book should come with a health warning: Do not read it if you don't want to connect more fully with Jesus and the amazing message of the cross! Reading this book is a must, whether you have been a Christian for a long time, want to understand Christianity more, or want to be able to help others connect with Jesus.

Sarah K. Belcher
Church Leader, Threshold, Lincolnshire

I loved reading *Same Cross New Questions*. I would recommend it to anyone who is keen to reflect on the significance of Christ's death and resurrection. I will be particularly recommending it to those who would like to become more effective in sharing Christ with others. My understanding of the cross has been enriched and I feel better equipped to help people from a variety of generations and backgrounds consider what has been accomplished through the cross.

Andy Barclay-Watt
Senior Leader, LifeChurch Manchester

A timely book! A conversation between friends that helps us find out what friendship with God could look like.

Anthony Delaney
Leader of Ivy Network churches, NewThing church planting, and LAUNCH conference

André has written a wonderful book that brings the Good News of Jesus to life in an original, fresh and accessible format. This is a resource that I will be recommending to young people in my church who want to grow in their understanding of the Christian faith and the incredible difference Jesus can make in their life. If you have questions about the meaning and significance of the cross, this book is an excellent place to start!

Rev. Danny Rodgers
Curate, Buckingham Parish Church

André's voice and passion for a deeply relational gospel shines through. I'm really encouraged by the dialogue he's promoting around understanding the richness of the cross for the emerging generation.

Alan Taylor
Fusion, Europe developer

This book really picks up on some very valuable points as to how to approach a person and talk about Christianity without coming across too strong or crazy. It's a good guide to help students and young adults talk about their faith with others, and for those who are struggling to incorporate God's love into their daily lives. It's also *really* quotable with interesting and unique descriptions of God and the cross. An extremely informative and fun book.

Efua Coleman
Leadership team, University of Salford Christian Union

André creates a caring conversation about how the cross can still speak into our feelings of worry, anxiety, loneliness and nagging belief that we are simply not good enough.

Ben Dyer
Young adults minister, Red Church, Ormskirk

This is an innovative approach to articulating theological truth for the digital native. André has successfully captured, in book form, what happens every day in ministry to young people and young adults: text chat. His articulation of the faith through these imaginary conversations is thoughtful, helpful and hopeful for pastors, youth leaders, student and young adult workers who are looking for new ways to engage today's culture, particularly when they are faced with questions about the cross. For anyone looking to 'connect' theology and the digital native, this book is a must-read.

Joseph Wood
Lecturer in Church History at Nazarene Theological College

The cross, even though it is the centre point of Christian faith, presents some of the deepest mysteries. No quicker are those mysteries discovered than in everyday conversations. What André does in this book is throw those ideas and conversations into the limelight and tackle the difficult questions that arise. It is both helpful and illuminating how André seeks to apply theology almost instantly. The conversations and scenarios are clearly birthed in real-life ministry moments, and to see how these central theological paradigms affect us is of such worth and necessary for those in everyday ministry. If you work with people who ask questions, this book is for you!

Rev. Alex Rayment
Church Leader and lecturer in Theology & Youth Ministry

Contents

Preface
Why did I write this book?

This book has been on my mind for a few years now. It's been bubbling up inside me because the more I think and reflect on Jesus, his life, death and resurrection, the more excited I am. I'm also humbled by it, and a passion keeps building in me as I realise again and again just how big and beautiful the gospel is. Jesus achieved so many different things when he died on the cross: he freed us from Satan's captivity, brought us into his family, brought us into a relationship with himself and fellow believers, demonstrated pure self-giving love, paid the price for all the times we don't follow God's holy law, and more besides. It's a wonderful gospel.

However, in my life I realised that there were times when I reduced this wonderful cross to one thing and one effect, and I saw this happening with friends and other people too. They knew God had forgiven them in a legal sense and declared them 'not guilty', but were struggling to believe the cross could overcome other problems they faced. Mainly, they struggled to believe that God wanted a relationship with them, that he was proud of them because of who they are rather than what they do, and that this relationship of unconditional love is real because of Jesus and his cross, that God sees the 'real us' and still sticks around in every situation.

A story involving a friend of mine best explains what I mean. A while ago, Alfie (not his real name) and I were catching up.

Alfie is in his mid-twenties and has been a Christian for more than ten years. He is a gifted evangelist and has led many people to God through preaching on stage and by talking to people in the pub, on the train, to his mates on his sports team, or wherever else he finds himself. He also did a gap year involving intense Christian mission. He has worked and volunteered for churches as a youth worker, community worker, and evangelist for a good few years now. He is someone I respect and who loves God and is trying to share his faith with others.

As we were talking, Alfie said he had struggled with insecurity, self-doubt and feeling unlovable for many years and had a very negative view of himself. He said that a few weeks ago his negative thoughts got really bad and he had been praying loads and crying out to God for help. After explaining his journey and the trials he faced, he said he now felt like he'd turned a corner and changed in a very radical way.

I asked him how this change had happened, and he said, 'I realised that God actually likes me. He likes spending time with me. He just actually likes me and wants a relationship with me.'

I was so happy that he realised this truth, but I was heartbroken too. This guy, who has led lots of people to God, has only just realised after ten years that God actually liked him. That through Jesus we get a close personal relationship with the living God who clears our debts but also brings us into his family. Who never loses patience or runs out of love for us, and will always be there. Who wants to connect and have a relationship with the real us. Why did it take him so long to really know and believe this truth? Why did it take him so long to see that the cross and resurrection can answer all the questions and struggles he faces?

14

The questions many people are asking nowadays, especially those of us from the younger generations and/or millennial generation, are similar to my friend's. Our deep struggles are around relationships: 'Am I loved?', 'Do I mean something to someone?', 'Does my life matter?' We struggle with loneliness, removing the (social media) mask and letting people see the real us. We worry that when we hit rock bottom, will anyone stick by us and love us through it all? Who can we really count on? Who can like me when I don't even like myself?

I wrote this book because I believe we can find answers to these questions in the life, death and resurrection of Jesus. I wrote this book to emphasise the biblical teaching that reveals the cross itself directly answers these questions and brings the deep connection and relationships we crave. I wrote this book to show how the theme of connection is often forgotten, but can enrich other amazing truths we know about the cross. I wrote this book because, whether we're Christians or not, I want to help expand our minds and hearts, and make more room for God and his beautiful gospel in our struggles and every area of our messy lives.

What's in this book?

This book is a bit different to other books about the cross. It involves a series of fictional conversation between Barney, the main character, and people linked to his church. These characters are trying to understand the life-changing power the gospel offers in the nitty-gritty of their hopes, pain, dreams, disappointments and everyday life. While Barney and the other characters are all fictional and not based on real people I know, the conversations are based on many real chats I've had with friends, family, people I've met, atheists, new Christians, old Christians and many other types of people too. The conversations are born out of real questions and real struggles.

I realise some of what I write will sound different to what we may be used to hearing. It may be challenging and/or very exciting. So at the end of each chapter I have written a few notes that highlight the key points and list some questions worth thinking about. I want it to help us process what we read and think about how we can apply it to our lives and contexts.

I could have written an essay-style book and just made my argument (which would have been much easier), but the power of the gospel is seen in changed lives. It's seen in everyday dialogue and the new decisions people make. As you read this book, I hope you find yourself engaging with the conversations, and let the dialogue and the discussions from Barney and the other characters resonate with the questions we can all find ourselves asking.

What are my hopes for this book?

I hope this book will allow us to have a firmer grasp on the gospel truth, God's love for us and his plans for us. I hope that through the conversations we read in this book, we will view the cross and resurrection with more joy and more hope, and believe even more that it can answer our deepest needs. I hope we are empowered to become more gospel-focused and to give God more space to build his kingdom through us and our everyday decisions. I pray above all that we realise, in a deeply radical and fresh way, just how much the cross and resurrection connects us to Jesus.

Prologue

'Can I belong?' Instead of 'Have I done wrong?'

PART 1

'People think the cross doesn't matter. They think Jesus is irrelevant. We all ask questions about who we really are, we search for our identity, how we fit in, and where we belong. Some people spend their whole lives asking these questions, but they overlook God because he's "outdated", right? Let's be honest, sometimes this is what *Christians* say, let alone everyone else. They just can't always see how God fits in, so they subconsciously look to other things.'

I look at her, wondering if she's taken in anything I've said. I know she is listening, but I'm not sure what she thinks of it all.

After a slight pause, she replies, 'You know, I respect you hugely, Barney, and I think the Bible has some good things in it but, on the whole, science has disproved it all. I mean, can you really believe that Jesus came back to life, or even existed, or that he was God, in this day and age? How can we know, anyway? We weren't there.'

Amy is a very warm person, polite and fun to be around, and I was surprised when she decided to come away to the big annual Christian festival our church group always goes to. Five days of camping in a semi-waterlogged field and eating from fast-food vans which have more grease than I care to think about. Twice a day we listened to Christian talks, then went to some seminars in-between, and sang worship songs. This had been our life for nearly every waking hour of the day in the past week. I assumed because she came she might have an interest in God, but I think she just wanted an excuse to go away with friends.

Amy carries on, in her polite manner: 'Don't get me wrong, I respect your opinion, and who am I to say you're wrong? I just think the whole Jesus thing isn't for me. I've just got this new promotion I worked really hard to get, and that's what gets me up in the morning. Not God.'

Anyone who talks to Amy is met with a very intelligent, hardworking, independent and stylish person. I think she sees us Christians as strange people who can't do life on their own and need help, although she would never say it that bluntly. She prefers to rely on herself and no one else.

'How many of the talks and preaches did you go to this week in the end, then?' I ask.

'I went to most of them, actually. I mean, I wasn't planning to, but most of my friends and people from our group went. I didn't want to sit in my tent on my own, there was no reception or Wi-Fi, so I tagged along.' She seems to want to emphasise that she was only *tagging along*. I don't draw attention to it.

'Which one did you find most interesting?' I go on.

'I liked the one about social justice: about Christians and the Church standing up to injustice in their communities and beyond. That other one, about God as a loving father and not just a distant judge was good. Really good, actually.' Her tempo picks up a bit. 'Oh, and the evening preach about how Jesus welcomes us into his family, as children of God. That was *really* interesting'. She suddenly realises that she is leaning forward and sits back quickly. 'Not that I cared too much, though. I mean, just thought those were better than most.' She clears her throat, picks up her phone and starts to scroll through it.

I look round at the rest of the group from my seat near the front. Different people catch my eye for different reasons, but here we all are, travelling back home on the coach together. I absolutely loved spending time with them and just hanging out together. Being at a festival with more than 5,000 other Christians can seem overwhelming at first, but it's great being around so many other believers. I managed to round up about thirty campers this year, mainly from our church, but some are friends of friends; some say they aren't even that interested in God.

I see that most people are chatting and making noise, others are in their own little worlds.

Amy puts her phone down and stares up at the ceiling of the coach. I turn away and look out of the window. I feel like there might be more going on with Amy than she's letting on. Maybe I'm just keen for her to see God how I see him. As a Saviour, a close friend, and loving father, whose death on the cross can transform our lives in the here and now and give us a sense of belonging and connection.

'So, why do you think those talks stood out to you, then?' I turn back and ask her.

She stays silent for a while, then slowly states: 'Well, at the start of the week I would have said I don't believe in God or Jesus, and I still don't. I was planning on just hanging out at our group's communal gazebo thing when the rest of you went to the talks. I just wanted to get away and relax for a few days, and

I love camping. But after going to a few talks, I got the sense that the people speaking wanted God to really affect their life. Like they wanted it to matter. It seemed to bring...purpose, I guess.'

Does my life matter? What's my purpose? Am I loved? The questions many people I work with ask, consciously or subconsciously, and get tied up in knots over. They exclude God from the questioning, the confusion, the insecurity everyone hides, and the shame these questions can bring when they can't answer them. Many are wrestling with these questions over years, decades even, and internalising the struggle, left believing no one else struggles like that. So we are then all left feeling we can't possibly talk about it.

'Hey, Barney.' I hear an excited voice come from over my shoulder as he runs down the aisle of the coach. That could only be Toby. 'I just had a few more questions to ask, can I sit here?' He is pointing to the empty seat across the aisle from us.

'Of course,' I reply. I fondly think of Toby as 'the ball of energy'. His enthusiasm is infectious. It's definitely risen even more since he became a Christian for the first time a few days ago. After all the struggles he has had in his life, it's great to see him so excited.

'So you said that...' Toby starts in an enthusiastic voice.

'There is no need to shout!' Amy says with a cheeky smile. She has come to really like Toby. They are both so outgoing. She calls him the little brother she always wanted. I think she likes the fact he's about to go to uni and is asking her and others what it's like. Getting their advice.

'Sorry,' he says in both a sarcastic and joking tone. 'I will try to speak with my "inside" voice,' he whispers. They look at each other and smile. 'Barney, you've worked for the church for a while, yeah? And you mainly support students and people in their twenties and thirties, yeah? And you said that you've discussed the cross and Jesus with many people, yeah?' He is speaking so quickly.

'Correct,' I reply, waiting for the real question. I love it, though. I love explaining what my faith means to me and how it can answer the issues we're facing today. It's great when someone like Toby is full of questions and so keen to discuss them.

'So the night I became a Christian, the preacher on the stage was talking about how Jesus died and was raised to life. The word is "resurrected", I think? Anyway, he said this dealt with our sin and mistakes. The preacher's story – about how he never had a good relationship with his dad, how he had been to prison, struggled with self-image and suicidal thoughts, but his relationship with God changed all that, even though he still isn't perfect – was so powerful. Bits of it really related to my life,' he says without flinching. He continues, speaking quickly, as if he needs to get it all out. 'I've been texting and messaging all my friends to tell them I'm a Christian now. And how it's because I now feel like God is real and he really does love me. Hearing all those stories about how Jesus was helping people, and when I was experiencing God's presence at the talks and in prayer and worship, it just made me feel connected and whole, you know? That's why I went forward to become a Christian that night. I wanted my own relationship with God.'

By this point his hands are flying round and the gesturing is getting bigger and bigger.

Toby keeps talking very quickly: 'I could see that my life could change, that I could belong and be real. I like people from your church – well, I guess it's *our* church now. I mean, I always enjoyed coming to your social event things for the last few months with mates. But I never thought this would happen. It just seems so strange, in a good way. I feel different. In a good way. I guess you can't really explain it, you know?'

'And your question?' I ask with a smile.

'Oh yeah.' He pauses for a bit. 'Yeah, right, erm. I wanted to ask, some mates here have been explaining what Jesus did on the cross and why he died. I want to make sure I understand. But I don't think I fully get it.' He pauses again. 'Is that OK with God? I do want to be a Christian, Barney, honest, but I'm worried if I don't understand it all God won't think I am. You know?'

'I think I understand what you mean,' I say.

'Do remember to breathe, Toby,' Amy says in a purposely slow and serious voice, which only emphasises the mockery. Toby glances at Amy and gives a half-smile, but he doesn't really respond. Not because he is offended, but he needs an answer. His hand gesturing reduces and his knee starts shaking.

'Let me make it clear,' I begin. 'No Christian understands God fully or has all the answers. We're all learning. I love it when people ask questions – when they try to understand Jesus more for themselves and think about how the cross can impact their lives. So asking questions is important, and this is a good one.' I go on. 'I don't think there is only *one* way to understand the cross. I think the authors of the Bible make it clear that Jesus' life, death and resurrection achieved many things. Each biblical picture, model and understanding of the cross looks at a different aspect, but all are just as important as the next. So we're always learning and discovering new truths that the Bible wants to teach us.'

'So I need to learn about more than one picture?' Toby says, a bit of worry creeping into his voice.

'You say *need* as if it's a jail sentence! What I mean is, Jesus achieved many things on the cross, and they're all wonderful and freeing and they allow us to live more authentically, be more real. The cross can help everyone with every aspect of life, it's not just a one-hit wonder.'[1]

Toby looks a bit puzzled.

'It's like a rainbow,' I continue. 'Each colour is beautiful on its own, but you can put all the colours together to make something even more spectacular. The cross is like that. Each aspect is individually stunning, but put them together and you see something even more amazing.'

'So how do you know which aspect to talk about, or think about?' Amy interjects.

'Well, different people need to hear different truths at different times, meaning we *emphasise* different things that Jesus achieved, depending on the context and need. It's vital to remember that the meaning of the cross is in the cross. The meaning isn't changing or defined by the context it's preached in, or in the needs of the hearers. But different objective and eternal truths are *emphasised* in different contexts so that different hearers can relate and know the cross can help them find answers.'[2]

'It's like saying: If someone needs to bang in a nail, we wouldn't help them by handing them a spanner. In any good toolbox we need a spanner, along with a drill and a tape measure, etc. They're all needed, but to bang in a nail you need a hammer. It's a bit like that with the cross because we need to help people by handing them the model and picture that addresses the problems they face.'[3]

'So the cross is like a multicoloured toolbox, it's both beautiful and useful?' Amy says, raising her eyebrows to stress the intended humour.

I laugh a bit, then say, 'I wasn't planning on putting it like that, but I guess that's right.'

'A multicoloured toolbox is one I may actually want to buy!' she says cheekily.

'So, erm, Jesus did more than one thing on the cross and it helps me, us, in many ways, but I don't need to worry about remembering it all now?' Toby says, with more hand gesturing and less knee twitching.

'Exactly. It's not a chore or a test. All Christians are learning more about God and building a deeper relationship. Ultimately, you just need to remember that Jesus died for you, for us, to save us and transform our lives and our purpose in many ways.'

'Sounds a bit too good to be true,' Amy says, straight-faced.

I can't quite work out what she means, but I reply, 'Well, we can't just tell people what they want to hear. I'll say it again, the context doesn't define or manipulate or change the meaning of the cross, but the context hugely impacts which aspect will be received with most openness. If we're handing people spanners when they need a hammer, then we aren't helping. They need a different tool from us. Do you see what I mean?'

They both nod.

'It's impossible to explain everything the cross achieved in one model or picture. That's why we need to listen to the need and respond wisely and sensitively with biblical truth, because one picture may be more relevant to someone in their context at that time. It doesn't mean the others pictures are untrue or unimportant. For example, I think many people I work with now are asking the question, "Can I belong?" instead of "Have I done wrong?" So the model and picture I often present for understanding the cross and resurrection focuses on that need, but it doesn't explain everything Jesus did. Just like a rainbow that has many complementary colours, Jesus' life, ministry, death and resurrection is so deep and rich that we need several complementary pictures and models to understand it all.'

'Well, I know God loves me, and his cross saves me, and I want to understand more,' Toby says whilst bouncing on his seat, smiling and waving his hands around. The ball of energy is alive and kicking again.

'You are such a child, Toby,' Amy says, smiling.

'We all know you love me deep down, sis,' Toby quickly throws back.

Amy rolls her eyes. 'You are annoying me today, like all little brothers.'

'I'm acting like I do every day.'

'You're right, you annoy me every day.'

Amy is far too quick for Toby, but he can take the banter. He enjoys it really. Besides, he has been too excited this week to let anything get him down for too long. After acknowledging she has got the better of him with a smile and a nod of the head, he suddenly jumps to his feet. 'I need to get my phone!'

he exclaims. He runs down the aisle to the back of the coach where he was previously sitting. I hear people calling after him as he passes them.

Amy looks down at her phone again, texting or doing something or other. I stare out the window and start thinking about the past week. So many Christians from our group, some of whom have apparently been going to church since they were in nappies, asked me many questions about faith and Christianity. I think it's really ironic that lots of them asked similar questions Toby just asked, and he only accepted Jesus into his life a few days ago.

I can see Amy is still on her phone. It looks quite intense. My guess is she's looking at work emails, as usual. She probably wants to get ahead on them before the Monday morning rush. I start to think about my work and how hectic it is. I don't even lead the church, I just look after students and those in their twenties and thirties, and that gives me more than enough to do. I couldn't imagine what it would be like to support everyone. But I enjoy focusing on the needs of our new, modern culture and giving people hammers instead of spanners. I want to show how God, Jesus and his cross are still useful and beautiful.

I see nothing of interest out of the window. I'm pleased the motorway doesn't have much traffic, though, which is fortunate considering it's summertime. I suddenly glimpse a lorry displaying the logo from our local supermarket, and I remind myself that I need to buy milk before I go home. My flat mate is away for two weeks so I know there won't be any there. Well, none I would like to drink, anyway. I wonder how he's doing. I hope he's left that DVD I want to watch. I could do with just sitting down and doing nothing tonight after I've unpacked. I should probably check my work emails too, but I'm so tired.

'Toby!' someone shouts from the back of the coach, followed by lots of loud laughter. Amy turns round and looks down the aisle, trying to see what is going on.

'Can you make out what's happening?' I ask Amy.

'Erm, no. I think he – actually, no, I can't see,' she says.

'No worries,' I reply.

Amy puts her phone down, no doubt distracted by the shouting from the back. She then looks at me suddenly. 'Barney,' she begins. 'You say the cross can answer all our questions. But most of the time you Christians say the cross forgives our sins, or whatever. But what if I don't need forgiveness because I feel like I've done nothing wrong? I don't break laws, so why do you lot say that?'

I pause for a second, then reply, 'Well, you're right, many Christians do start there. But there is a big assumption you and they're making, which is that this "forgiveness of sins" only falls into a legal framework. You said, "I've done nothing wrong" – you assume sin is only about breaking the rules. You're right, though, Christians will often say something like: we sin when we break God's law and should be punished, but when we have a relationship with Jesus we're being found "not guilty". We're avoiding punishment because Jesus took our punishment on the cross. In the not too distant past, people used to worry a lot about being "found guilty" and getting forgiveness in the "legal" sense. This is why many Christians are used to starting with an answer for that question.[4] But while I totally believe Jesus did bring this type of forgiveness on the cross and this is very important, the cross and forgiveness of sins also goes beyond this legal understanding too. We need to get underneath the assumptions we hold and realise there are other tools in the multicoloured toolbox. There is more than one colour in the rainbow.'

'So what do you think forgiveness means, then? It must be about breaking a rule. What else could it mean?'

'I think a very helpful definition of forgiveness is "to wipe the slate clean". Forgiveness of sins wipes the slate clean and this simultaneously deals with many aspects, like our past mistakes and future possibilities. Put it like this – when a friend truly forgives me when I make a mistake, it doesn't just mean they no longer hold a grudge, it also means we can be friends again. In other words, my friend forgives me in the "legal" sense and deals with my guilt and decides not to punish me, even though I deserve it. At the same time, reconciliation is taking place and our relationship is being restored. Forgiveness means lots of things are happening at once, the slate being wiped clean in many ways.'

'So what would you say to someone who said they don't think they need Jesus?'

'Well, it depends. If people do feel they've done something wrong and broken God's law, the cross completely deals with that need, so I would start there. But there is more to it, so if people only come to God for dealing with guilt, then something is wrong. If people use internet search engines to find knowledge and ignore the cross in their search for knowledge, then something is wrong. If people go to the local community club to understand friendship, belonging and connection, and think the cross is useless in this area, then something is wrong. If people join activist groups to understand how to fight injustice and overlook the cross, then something is wrong. Obviously, all of these things are good and can be part of the answer, even a vital part, but the cross is more than a "get out of jail free" card. If I, as a Christian, cannot articulate how the cross answers the other questions people are asking, then I haven't grasped its depth. "Forgiveness of sins" means more than one thing, the cross achieves more than one thing. Like I said, in my experience people are often now asking "Can I belong?" rather than "Have I done wrong?" I really believe that's why it's necessary to keep thinking about how we communicate Jesus' message to each generation because I truly believe that the cross, resurrection, life and ministry of Jesus can answer every human need at any given time. We just need to show why that's true.'

She pauses for a second and goes to speak, but before we can carry on, the coach turns into a service station.

PART 2

'Sorry,' I say before standing up. 'We can keep chatting later. I really would like to chat more about this. Put it on hold for a bit.'

'Yeah, sure,' she says, in her polite and understanding manner.

'Right, everyone,' I try to shout over the noise of the coach. 'We're going to make a pit stop, only a quick one though, still got a long way to go. Please be back in thirty minutes. I'll stay with the coach, so you can leave belongings here if you want.'

People begin to get up and the general chaos of looking for jumpers, shoes, bags and wallets ensues. The gentle tap on the shoulder to wake up those who have fallen asleep. People taking out their headphones to ask someone what's happening. I enjoy it so much! The chaos of being a group and creating a family. It's sad the week is coming to an end.

Amy grabs her bag and walks off the coach. Others are walking past me to get off the coach too, double-checking with me how long they have. I can see Toby bouncing down the aisle as well.

'Barney, I just messaged my best mate. We're meeting up later and going for a drink. I want to tell him about Jesus.'

'Sounds good,' I remark.

'Can we chat later about what I should say, yeah? I'm not sure where to begin, you know?'

'Just tell him why you decided to become a Christian. What's changed. That you know God loves you. Just be honest, it's your story. But you need to keep moving, you're holding everyone up!' I gesture to those behind him.

'Oh right – sorry, everyone!' he shouts back down the aisle before scrambling off the coach.

As I wait for everyone to leave, I see Tina get up. Tina is shy. She has come out of her shell a lot during the week, but still prefers to be in the company of a few rather than in a big crowd. She is very thoughtful, measured, and you can tell she cares about people. Always looks a bit anxious though, as if she has 1,000 questions racing around her head, worried that if she asks them, people will judge her.

'Hi, Tina, you all right?' I ask.

'Barney, is it OK if I stay here and chat with you?' she says without making much eye contact.

'Of course – are you sure you don't want anything?'

'No, I would prefer to stay.'

I have no idea why she wants to stay. She is so hard to read. Most people had left, with the exception of two sleepers at the back, a gentle snore coming from one of them, and a few others who are dotted around, deciding to stay and keep chatting and/ or playing on their phones. Tina and I sit down.

'I hope you enjoyed the week. I'm really happy you decided to become a Christian again after all of these years,' I tell her.

Apparently, Tina grew up going to Sunday school and went to church a bit as a teenager. That was more than fifteen years ago now. All this was way before my time at the church, and Tina is the sort of person who gives very little away. I think some people let her down at church and hurt her in the past. She has been coming back sporadically for the last few months.

'I do plan on coming to church more regularly. I want to make sure I come.'

'That's good. It's great having you as part of the family. I've enjoyed getting to know you this week; everyone else has too. And the cakes that you baked and brought along were incredible.'

'Thanks, and sorry if I've asked too many questions this week.'

'I honestly don't mind. I'm happy to try to answer them.' I have a feeling that there is a deep question Tina is preparing to ask, but she doesn't know how to ask it. Getting stuff out of her is tricky.

'How are you feeling about becoming a Christian again?' I say.

'I feel different. I do feel happy. I kinda stopped believing in God for all those years, but hearing about Jesus again, and what he did on the cross after all this time, I really feel like I used to feel. I feel like he's real and loves me.' She started to fidget. 'But, do you believe ...' She looks down at the floor. '... that Jesus can know us individually, and he really wants a relationship with us?'

'Yes, I do,' I reply instantly. 'I believe God does loves us and wants to have a relationship with us. That's one reason why Jesus died on the cross, so that we could relate to him. We were separated from God, so Jesus, who is God, died and was resurrected to overcome the separation and establish a loving relationship with us again.'

'But there are so many people, why would God care about everyone? He must have lots of other things on his mind. Why would he notice me?' Her eyes open wide, as if she has revealed something by mistake. 'I mean, *us* – how do we know God cares about any one person?'

I can tell that this question means a lot to her. She told me earlier in the week I could pray for her work situation. One of the few things she asked for prayer for. She's working with some really difficult colleagues and hates confrontation. Not exactly easy. She wants to know God sees that situation. She needs to know he cares, even when she doesn't fit in, feels like an outsider and feels like she doesn't belong. At least, I think that's what she is getting at, anyway.

I look at her and try to help. 'Tina, God loves you, he wants to know you. He wants you to know him. He wants to be there with you every step of the way. He wants a relationship and we can know that because of the cross. God sees the "backstage of

Tina's life" and is interested. He's not just interested in the front stage glamour.'

She takes a deep breath. 'It's just that last night the preacher was talking about how Jesus died for our sins and so now we're found "not guilty". I believe that's true, but what really spoke to me was when he said God is a loving father. God cares about us and wants to know us. He'll be there when no one else is. It was like the person on stage was speaking to just me.' Her voice trails off at the end slightly.

I reply gently but firmly. 'Tina, God is bigger and greater than we can imagine, yet he wants to know us individually. It's amazing, really. He wants to know you and build a relationship with you. He is like that friend who always gets you a birthday card when others forget, asks how you are, remembers the little things you like and don't like, and always greets you with a smile. And I believe this is only possible because Jesus died for our sins.'

She is looking at me more now, so I continue: 'In all the work I do with young adults, people are often asking the same kind of questions you are. You're not alone. They ask things like: "Am I loved?" or "Does my life matter?" or "Am I worth something to someone?" They want to know someone really cares and will really stick around, but they aren't sure how Jesus dying on the cross and the Bible can help them. And I'm talking about people in our church!'

She is still looking and taking it all in. I go on. 'I gave a talk at church last month, I called it the *Connection Atonement Model*. I was explaining how we can take these questions our culture is asking and answer them with what the Bible says about Jesus' death and resurrection. How we can emphasise a particular, but no less biblical, understanding of the cross, sin, and forgiveness, to meet people where they're at. We may be asking new questions, but the cross has always offered us the answers.'

'I wasn't at that talk, sorry,' she says softly.

'There's no need to apologise. You say sorry too much; it wasn't your fault you weren't there!'

'I know I do, sorry. I don't mean that, well, I do, but . . . ' We both chuckle a bit, which breaks the tension. She looks away again. 'You know what I mean.'

'Well, this Connection Model is based in a very relational context, and emphasises God as a loving father, Jesus as loving friend, and the cross as welcoming us into a family. But using these concepts to explain the cross isn't new. Many other Church leaders and theologians talk about it, and I was trying to pull together a lot of ideas that are already out there.[5] For example, the Reconciliation Model focuses on the relational problems the cross overcomes. Although, it primarily talks about broken relationships from God's viewpoint, and I explained that this connection understanding is subtly different and starts from our viewpoint.'

She looks like she is trying to processes all of this, but I continue anyway: 'Look, what I'm trying to say is that in my talk I wanted to show that the cross itself can offer us purpose and identity, deal with our individual shame and bring us into loving relationships with God and others. How it can answer the relational questions our culture seems to be asking, and what you're asking me.'

'I'm quite creative and visual, so I work better with pictures, but I sort of get it,' Tina says, unconvincingly.

'Well, then, imagine you, or somebody, is trapped on an island and they're all alone. The island is very nice, most people would call it paradise and say they're lucky to be there. But that person just wants someone to notice them. To hear them when they call out. To come along and connect with them. That's how they would get "saved" in that situation. This picture of the cross is a bit like that. That islander isn't calling for legal forgiveness or triumph over evil in that moment. They are *screaming* out for someone to notice and connect with them and save them from isolation. From feeling absent. They are *yearning* for someone to hear them and be with them in their struggle, first and foremost.'

Tina looks directly at me, intrigued, I think. Just as I'm about to ask her if she got it, she begins: 'OK, I think I see what you mean now.' She goes on, 'You really believe that God sees our situation, knows us individually, and can brings us out of isolation and into a loving relationship because of what Jesus did? The cross brings a connection over the disconnection. Is that right?'

'Yeah, exactly,' I say.

'So it was like God was speaking to just me last night, like that friend who really cares and greets me with a smile.' Tina responds whilst giving more eye contact and speaking a bit louder.

'Correct. He can relate to us because of Jesus' life and death, and show us we are loved, that we mean something, and that our life matters.'

Tina leans back; she looks more at peace.

Suddenly a loud noise goes off and I nearly jump out of my seat. It's my mobile phone and it really startles me. After camping in a field for five days with barely any signal or Wi-Fi, texts and notifications seem like a distant memory. Hearing it gives me a shock. Tina laughs at me. 'You must know what your own phone sounds like,' she jokes.

'You would hope so,' I say, a bit embarrassed. 'It's Toby.' I read it and smile. 'Listen to this, he says some of them are buying a coffee and are discussing something and he wants to know what I think. He clearly can't wait till he gets back to the coach.'

'That sounds about right,' she says in a friendly tone. 'He is one of a kind. What does he want to know?'

'People here are saying Jesus died for our sins. So I want to know, what exactly is the definition of "sin"?'

Tina looks like she is thinking about it.

'That is a great question,' I say, 'and something that definitely needs more attention . . .'

AUTHOR'S NOTES

I realise that by now you may be starting to feel a bit overwhelmed. I've thrown a lot at you so far, and Barney has made a lot of different points in his conversations. You may be feeling excited, curious, unsure, all the above, or something else entirely.

So I wanted to add a few personal comments, which I will do at the end of each chapter, to highlight a few points. I hope it will help you to process everything that's been said.

No matter what your belief is, I hope that by thinking these things through you get fired up about Jesus and what his death and resurrection achieved.

Key Takeaways

- The cross is like a multicoloured toolbox; it's beautiful and useful in many different ways.

- The cross brings forgiveness of sins, which 'wipes the slate clean' and does many things at once. It isn't only about being declared 'not guilty' in a legal sense.

- Different people have different starting points, questions and problems. By *emphasising* different aspects of the cross and resurrection, we can talk about Jesus to these multiple groups and people in our culture.

- Nowadays lots of people are asking, in one way or another, 'Can I belong?' Instead of 'Have I done wrong?'

Real Life Stories

I remember going to a big Christian festival a few years after I became a Christian. The keynote speaker, who I respected a lot, said that he tried to talk to his relative and their spouse about Jesus. But they said they were 'good people' and didn't feel too bad about anything. The speaker then said that although we've all done bad things, because they didn't acknowledge it, he didn't know how to talk about Jesus. The speaker then said he wanted them to do something terrible, or commit a crime, so big that they had to see how bad it was so that Jesus could become relevant.

I was shocked.

An influential, keynote Christian speaker, basically told us 5,000 or so people at the festival that God can only impact your life if you think you've done something bad or commit a crime. It's only when we feel we've broken a rule that God can possibly step in. As if the cross and resurrection isn't relevant or helpful in any other situation. I went away very upset by it.

Fast forward many years – when I was thinking about writing this book and explaining the idea to a friend, she started getting very animated. She said that very week she was talking to her friends who didn't believe in God, and they said to her that she was always trying to get them to admit they were 'bad' people. They always got annoyed and thought God was just an angry God who was desperate to punish everyone.

These stories really remind me that some people are standing in a different starting point. And unless Christians in the Church can find a way to communicate how big and wide the effects of the cross are, in a way that meets people where they're at, everyone will just keep getting frustrated.

Real Life Application

You may have never gone to church, or you may have been more than a million times. Either way, we can often put God in a box. We can assume the cross can help us in one area, like when we feel bad after doing something, but not really help when we think about other things, like belonging or connection.

This chapter was getting us to think about the possibility of the cross and resurrection being about more than one thing. How we could potentially let it play a bigger role in our life if we want it to. How we can look to the cross to answer every need, and our biggest need, instead of reducing it to a one-hit wonder.

The rest of this book is going to focus on the 'connection' idea that Barney spoke about, and how this perspective could enrich other amazing truths we know about the cross and resurrection.

At this point, I think some good questions to ask yourself are:

- What words do I use to describe the effects of the cross?

- To what extent do I think these words impact my daily life and needs?

Further Reading

Blocher, H., 'Biblical Metaphors and the Doctrine of Atonement', *JETS* 47/4 (December 2004), 629-645.

Holmes, S.R., *The Wondrous Cross: Atonement and Penal Substitution in the Bible and History*, Milton Keynes: Paternoster, 2007.

Schmiechen, P., *Saving Power: Theories of Atonement and Forms of the Church*, Grand Rapids, MI: Eerdmans, 2005.

Williams, R., *God With Us: The Meaning of the Cross and Resurrection. Then and Now*, London: SPCK, 2017.

Chapter 1

'How do I talk about sin?'
Christ came to connect

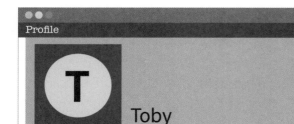

Profile

T

Toby

Age 18

Work/Education
First year at uni, studying Media and Performance.

About me
Love my coffee, love my church, and love useless facts... when I remember them!

You'll probably find me acting, playing darts, or visiting new places. I don't like being on my own, so always happy to hang out if you're free! Shout out to my mum who did a stunning job raising me and my brothers.

Jesus is my homeboy, wouldn't trade him in for anything, bro!

What's the one question you would ask God?
Who can I tell about Jesus?

Current status
Awkward when you realise you're not an evangelist after all.

Part 1

B Hello Toby, hope you're settling into uni and getting on with people in your halls. Just seen your status, you OK? I tried to call a few times but no answer. Just wanted to send you a quick message. Let me know how you are.

T Hi Barney, great to hear from you. Yeah, sorry, I can't really call right now. Me and some mates are watching the game in our local and I wouldn't be able to hear you in here. I've just been getting a round in. So many of us, so expensive!

B Don't worry about it. I won't call or keep messaging you if you're busy, but I just want to make sure you're OK. I saw your status. I'm assuming you've had some tough conversations?

T Messaging is fine, mate. I'm not that into footy anyway. I just don't want to miss out on the socialising! It's been a bit tough, in all honesty. I was really excited about coming to uni and sharing my story and telling people about God, but some of them are reacting badly.

The problem is, a lot of people say they don't want to hear that they're 'guilty', or a 'sinner', so I don't know how to tell them about Jesus or the cross.

B What do you mean by that?

T Well, I tell them that we're all sinners, me included, and we're all guilty and have done stuff wrong, but Jesus died for our sins to save us. But they basically say things like 'I'm not a bad person' or 'You can't just tell people their bad, it's all subjective'.

B I see. Has this happened a lot, then?

T Yeah. I've had good conversations too, you know me, always talking about God now. But one guy got really, really upset. He basically screamed at me and was like, 'I've done nothing wrong. Why do you Christians want to say I'm a bad person? I give to charity! I'm a nice person!' I felt really bad about it.

The problem is, when I say we've all sinned because we all break God's law, they often switch off or get upset. I just want them to see Jesus how I see him. I can share my story, but I don't know how to talk about sin and stuff with them.

B Sorry to hear that, mate. Sorry it's got you down. Those conversations can be tough. But it sounds like you want them to admit they're guilty, and the assumption is they will agree with your set of rules and laws and that they've done stuff wrong. Why is that your starting point?

T Well, Jesus died on the cross to forgive our sins, because we've broken his rules, so that's what they need to know, right?

B I agree that the cross does bring forgiveness of sins, but this forgiveness isn't only referring to a 'legal' forgiveness or a 'not guilty' verdict. This isn't the only thing the cross brings. I think the cross achieves more than one thing. Do you remember, I've said this before?

T No, not really, sorry.

B Sure you do, we said it's like a multicoloured toolbox. On the coach?

T Oh yeah, how could I forget that! Yeah yeah, and the Bible has many pictures to explain the cross, they're all useful and beautiful. Yeah I do, I remember now.

B I also said we *emphasise* different aspects depending on the context. What we say about the cross needs to be rooted in the Bible, but different hearers may need to hear different aspects about the cross.

T I'm not sure I'm following you. Surely as a Christian, I'm trying to make Jesus relevant to non-

Christians, so I need to show them they're guilty of sinning, but it's OK because Jesus has a solution.

B Well, put it like this. Imagine someone comes over to your house and sees your massive DVD collection. All your cabinets are filled with DVDs and you even have lots of movies online too. Then you pick up an action film, but they say they don't like action movies. What would you do?

T Suggest a different film, probably.

B Exactly, you wouldn't say, 'We need to watch this action film, it has the best reviews.' Then after they say no again, you wouldn't keep saying, 'But I don't think you understand, this film is a great film', and so on. Why would you ignore the other movies in your house?

T What does that have to do with Jesus and the cross?

B Everything! Jesus did so much on the cross and achieved so many things to help humanity because he loves us. So if someone says 'guilt' isn't their main concern or problem, you don't need to keep saying the same thing or 'Well, I don't think you understand'. You can look at other effects, you can watch other DVDs.

T But I feel you're talking about the starter before the main course. At the end of the day, the cross is all about sin, so people need to know they've broken God's law.

B Well, there's your problem; you think sin is *only* about breaking God's law. I believe forgiveness of sin is about 'wiping the slate clean'. Yes, we're declared 'not guilty' at the cross and resurrection and that's important, but there are so many more rich and wonderful things happening too. Things people may want to hear about.

Most Christians try to show people they've done something wrong. They do this tactfully, or even harshly. But I suggest maybe we can *emphasise* a different aspect of the cross so that they can understand God better, and experience him and know him more.

Yes, we've broken God's law, yes we're guilty, but if someone is at a different starting point asking different questions, then let's meet them at their need. We can bring them to the cross by emphasising a different truth. One that's relevant and will transform their lives.

T But I don't get it, how else can I talk about sin and being a sinner?

B Let's talk about the assumptions behind your chats. What would you say if I asked (I think you asked me this before but we didn't get a chance to talk about it properly): How would you define sin?

T I think I would still say, and people have told me, that sin is breaking God's law and not following his rules for our life. There are commands set by God and actions that are wrong. Like murder, gossiping, stealing, etc., so when we break God's law we sin. This separates us from God, who wants to love us but can't because of our sin.

B So put simply, sin is the 'bad stuff' we do?

T Yeah, I guess so. It's breaking his rules. Missing the mark.

B So then the cross, Christianity, overcoming sin, is all about not doing 'bad stuff'. Therefore salvation, or living a good Christian life, means not doing 'bad stuff', not breaking God's laws.

T Yeah, kind of.

B So imagine being locked in your room all day every day. If you sat in your room, never spoke to anyone or connected with anyone, but therefore didn't lie, gossip, forget to pray, murder anyone, and didn't even have bad thoughts, that would be a great Christian life? After all, you wouldn't be doing 'bad stuff'.

T That doesn't feel quite right.

B Exactly. Christianity must be about more than not doing 'bad things'. Where does love, joy, peace and happiness fit into that idea? There must be more, the gospel of 'good news' must be about more. Forgiveness wipes the slate clean and surely offers more than 'bad stuff' avoidance.

T But doing bad things needs to be avoided, right?

B Definitely, but that's not all we do as Christians. It's our job and honour to communicate to people how big God is and how great the gospel message is. Remember, it's like a rainbow that's made up of many beautiful colours; the gospel, the cross, the resurrection are made up of many beautiful things, not just one thing.

T What does this have to do with people shouting at me? How can I talk about sin and Jesus with them?

B Well, you need to understand that eighty years ago, society on the whole believed there was one ultimate truth. But nowadays people tend to think everyone can find their own truth. There isn't one ultimate right answer anymore. You've heard words or phrases like relativism, individualism, or 'do whatever makes you happy'.

T Yeah, the idea that tolerance is king. Everyone can have their own beliefs, no one wants to judge people. That kind of thing, right? I get so worried about offending people sometimes, but I always put my foot in it!

B Therefore, if people think truth is relative, how can you say to someone there is one ultimate law, one ultimate rulebook, one ultimate right and wrong, and you've broken it? You would be starting from different places. People don't automatically believe one God, one religion and one law is correct anymore.

Many Christians are trying to take people to *their own* starting point. Namely that we've all broken God's law, which is part of sinning. But nowadays most people's starting point is different. So why not go to their starting point and understand their needs, rather than dragging them to ours?

We can start with a different DVD. And *emphasise* a different colour in the rainbow.

T I am well confused! If you're trying to say that we need to have a different starting point, then what is it? And how does it affect how we see sin?

B Well, I would say it starts with the Bible. We can't just make something up. However, we need to understand culture too, and communicate in a way that impacts people's needs.

T OK, so how can I find people's starting point?

B Well, we listen to them, and I think many people are asking, 'Am I loved?', 'Am I alone?', 'Is my life worth something?', 'Where can I belong?' Their starting point is about isolation, disappointment and finding acceptance.

I would also say that in the Bible sin can be defined as: disconnection or dysfunctional relationships. This results in things like shame, isolation and feeling unworthy.

So this starting point overlaps with emphasising sin as disconnection. By understanding sin in this way, it can allow us to meet people where they're at and talk about God in a way that seems relevant, in a way that speaks to their situation and need.

T I think I was actually asking those questions before I became a Christian, and even now, if I'm honest. I was finding it hard to live up to my social media 'always happy' profile. I was looking for someone to say they liked the real me.
I found it hard to show people the real me, and find meaning in my life. I still struggle with it.

When I became a Christian, the preacher was talking about knowing God and being connected to him and him loving me. I mean, me?! It made me feel accepted. Wanted. I just want people to feel like this, too. It's frustrating that I can't get them to see God in this way.
I feel like a fraud sometimes.

B Join the club, Toby! We all feel like we're not good enough, which is partly why we're trying to find acceptance. I feel like this, too.

T Really, no! You mean you get this feeling as well?

B Yes, I do. But I think the Bible has an answer for us in this place. When we look at the Bible, which is our foundation, we can see sin being defined as relational dysfunction. We all sin, we cause it and are affected by it, and Jesus meets us in that place and overcomes it.

But if sin is understood as dysfunctional relationships, and people disconnecting, then in that context, telling people they're bad and do bad things is very unhelpful. People know life can be rubbish, they realise they aren't perfect, they don't need to be told they're wrong but that they can still connect.

People don't want more death, they want more life.

T I mean, thinking about it, I see it here at uni, and in my church up here, too. People are desperate to connect, be liked, feel part of the group. They even act differently around different people and pretend they have it all sorted. They only put the good things on social media, not the struggles.

B We see loneliness on the rise in our culture too.[1] Broken families, people moving round and losing touch with friends. People feeling unlovable, ugly, not feeling unique enough, and comparing themselves to everyone. They feel like people won't like the real them, they're unable to connect properly and reveal who they really are.

T And the Bible says that sin is relational dysfunction and disconnection, yeah? And that

> this causes shame, feeling unworthy, isolation, broken relationships, that sort of stuff?

B It doesn't give a definition in a 'dictionary' sense, but we see this idea at the very start of the Bible story in Genesis. This is because Adam and Eve are in a loving connected relationship with God and each other in Genesis 1 and 2 before sin enters the world.

Genesis 1:27-28

So God created [humans] in his own image, in the image of God he created them; male and female he created them. God blessed them and said to them, 'Be fruitful and increase in number; fill the earth and subdue it. Rule over the fish in the sea and the birds in the sky and over every living creature that moves on the ground.'

Genesis 1:31

God saw all that he had made, and it was very good. And there was evening, and there was morning – the sixth day.

Genesis 2:25

Adam and his wife were both naked, and they felt no shame.

The first few chapters of the Bible make it clear that loneliness and disconnection aren't part of God's desire for us. What we see is that Adam and Eve are fully connected to God and each other. There's no shame and no barriers. They lived in good relationship together before sin entered the world.[2]

T Oh yeah, I have read this chapter with a friend from my uni church. Then Adam and Eve ate the forbidden fruit and sin came into the world.

B Indeed. And what we see is that this sin brings disconnection and broken relationships. Adam and Eve feel shame and cover up. They hide from God and are separated from him. They blame each other. In other words, they begin to relate differently and hide who they really are; they begin to feel unworthy around others. They begin to disconnect.

Genesis 3:7-8

Then the eyes of both of them were opened, and they realised they were naked; so they sewed fig leaves together and made coverings for themselves. Then the man and his wife heard the sound of the Lord God as he was walking in the garden in the cool of the day, and they hid from the Lord God among the trees of the garden.

Genesis 3:12-13

The man said, 'The woman you put here with me – she gave me some fruit from the tree, and I ate it.' Then the Lord God said to the woman, 'What is this you have done?' The woman said, 'The snake deceived me, and I ate.'

Genesis 3:23

So the Lord God banished him from the Garden of Eden to work the ground from which he had been taken.

T So sin is disconnection, which brings alienation, blame, feeling shame, emptiness, loneliness, and absentness?

B Yes, Adam and Eve had decided to relate to God in a different way and not the way God asked. They decided not to trust him or build a good relationship. They decided not to love God fully or relate to him in a loving, trusting way. They stopped doing what was needed to make the relationship strong. It's a relational context.

Genesis 2:17

[God said] but you must not eat from the tree of the knowledge of good and evil, for when you eat from it you will certainly die.

Genesis 3:4-6

'You will not certainly die,' the snake said to the woman. 'For God knows that when you eat from it your eyes will be opened, and you will be like God, knowing good and evil.' When the woman saw that the fruit of the tree was good for food and pleasing to the eye, and also desirable for gaining wisdom, she took some and ate it. She also gave some to her husband, who was with her, and he ate it.

Genesis 3:9-10

But the Lord God called to the man, 'Where are you?' He answered, 'I heard you in the garden, and I was afraid because I was naked; so I hid.'

Disconnection is relating unloving. We feel isolation, unlovable, separated. But we also reject God and don't love him fully. We hurt others because we don't love fully, we sin against God and others.

So you could say anything short of a loving relationship is sin. Jesus himself said the greatest commandment isn't a list of rules, but simply love God with everything and love your neighbour as yourself. If we relate to God and others with love, putting their needs first, then we don't sin. Another very relational context and emphasis.

Mark 12:28-31

One of the teachers of the law came and heard them debating. Noticing that Jesus had given them a good answer, he asked him, 'Of all the commandments, which is the most important?' 'The most important one,' answered Jesus, 'is this: "Hear, O Israel: The Lord our God, the Lord is one. Love the Lord your God with all your heart and with all your soul and with all your mind and with all your strength." The second is this: "Love your neighbour as yourself." There is no commandment greater than these.'

You mean that if we don't relate to someone lovingly, like when we use people or do something selfish or out of hate, out of disconnection, then that brings alienation, shame, isolation and stuff? When relationships are dysfunctional, then that's sinning?

B Exactly. Sin can be seen as people taking their eyes off God and their neighbour and relating unlovingly to them. They start to think about themselves and ignore God and others, or use others for their own benefit.[3] It's a broken relationship.

This can happen in the big things (like murder) or the small things (like cancelling on a friend because a better offer came up). It's all relational dysfunction.[4]

---

2 Corinthians 5:14-15

For Christ's love compels us, because we are convinced that one died for all, and therefore all died. And he died for all, that those who live should no longer *live for* themselves *but for him who died for them and was raised again.*

T So people stop looking outwards, decide not to relate or follow God, and look inwards, and so disconnection happens right?

B This makes even more sense when you read the end of the Bible, where it talks about eternity and what happens after we die. It says sin and the suffering it causes will be wiped out. God will relate and connect with his people without any barriers. A new heaven and earth will come and there will be good fully loving relationships.

Revelation 21:1-4

Then I saw 'a new heaven and a new earth,' for the first heaven and the first earth had passed away, and there was no longer any sea. I saw the Holy City, the new Jerusalem, coming down out of heaven from God, prepared as a bride beautifully dressed for her husband. And I heard a loud voice from the throne saying, 'Look! God's dwelling-place is now among the people, and he will dwell with them. They will be his people, and God himself will be with them and be their God. "He will wipe every tear from their eyes. There will be no more death" or mourning or crying or pain, for the old order of things has passed away.'

So the Bible starts and ends with a time where there is/will be no sin. Good, loving relationships between God and us, and each other, exist. God lives and walks with us and there is no barrier. Jesus tells his followers to create loving relationships because the way we relate to God and others is the most important thing.

This would mean that connection is what God desires with us and between us. Sin brings disharmony, shame and separation instead of good relationships. Feeling safe, secure, loved and interconnected is replaced by blame, isolation and unworthiness. Sin is relating unlovingly. Sin is disconnection.

T So this is what I need to remember about sin, then?

B Like I always say, the cross does more than one thing, and sin can be defined biblically in more than one way. The gospel's impact and defeating of sin is like a beautiful rainbow. But one vital aspect and definition of sin is disconnecting from a full relationship with God and others.

T But couldn't you say that this is still a list of bad things, then? Relating badly and disconnection happens because people do 'bad stuff'. And you said sin isn't meant to be understood as a list of bad things.

B If someone lights a firework and you're standing far back at a safe distance, you only see it shoot up and explode. You don't see the fuse being lit. I think sin is the fuse, and the explosion is the 'bad stuff'. We can see the explosion and the effects but not what causes it. I think the cause in this case, the sin, is the relational dysfunction.

In other words, 'bad things' happen because we're not connecting. Sin occurs when we don't reach God's desire for us. Namely, good relationships that are free from shame and have true connections. So when we don't love our neighbour, *then* we lie or cheat. When we feel shame and disconnection, *then* we gossip or murder.

Look, having rules is important, but Jesus' greatest commandment (and I see the irony, calling it a 'command') teaches us that if we're relating to God and our neighbour with love, then all the 'rules' will naturally be followed. Nothing would go wrong. Selfless, loving relationships free from sin lead to no 'bad stuff'.

T

Or to put it another way, too much selfie isn't healthy?

B

Ha ha, that's a good one. Did you just come up with that? Yeah, we need to stop looking at ourselves too much and look to God and others. Sin is when we fall short of loving God and our neighbour fully, when we don't relate as God intended.

People become separated and alienated from God. They are disconnected from him and the life he wants them to have.

T

Would the 10 Commandments be an example of the effects of sin, then? If we aren't loving our neighbour, we commit adultery. Or when we aren't loving God fully, we may not make time for him, or worship other gods more, right? I think it says something like that anyway.[5]

B Good shout. Idolatry, not giving God your full heart, was always warned against in the Bible.[6] God was always trying to connect fully. Even the Exodus story, where God brought slaves out of Egypt to the promised land, wasn't really about getting to a location, but God bringing his people back to himself and trying to connect.

Exodus 19:4-6

'You yourselves have seen what I did to Egypt, and how I carried you on eagles' wings and brought you to myself. Now if you obey me fully and keep my covenant, then out of all nations you will be my treasured possession. Although the whole earth is mine, you will be for me a kingdom of priests and a holy nation.' These are the words you are to speak to the Israelites.

People sometimes miss the fact that the 10 Commandments came after God had saved the Israelites from slavery. Which is important because it shows that God's grace, love and desire to connect came before anything else. God made the first move.

T I never thought of it like that before.

B There is a constant thread, a constant theme in the Bible, which emphasises fully connected loving relationships. Sin is falling short of that. Sin is disconnection.

In the first part of the Bible, which is often called the Old Testament and was written before Jesus came down to Earth, God is constantly being faithful and trying to forge a relationship with his people.

Even though they constantly rejected him, worshipped other gods, acted like God didn't exist and they didn't deserve God's love, in the end God still sticks with them.

Isaiah 1:2-19

Hear me, you heavens! Listen, earth! For the Lord has spoken: 'I reared children and brought them up, but they have rebelled against me. The ox knows its master, the donkey its owner's manger, but Israel does not know, my people do not understand.' Woe to the sinful nation, a people whose guilt is great, a brood of evildoers, children given to corruption! They have forsaken the Lord; they have spurned the Holy One of Israel and turned their backs on him . . . Come now, let us settle the matter,' says the LORD. *'Though your sins are like scarlet, they shall be as white as snow; though they are red as crimson, they shall be like wool. If you are willing and obedient, you will eat the good things of the land . . .*

Hosea 11:1-11

When Israel was a child, I loved him, and out of Egypt I called my son. But the more they were called, the more they went away from me. They sacrificed to the Baals and they burned incense to images . . . My people are determined to turn from me. Even though they call me God Most High, I will by no means exalt them. 'How can I give you up, Ephraim? How can I hand you over, Israel? How can I treat you like Admah? How can I make you like Zeboyim? My heart is changed within me; all my compassion is aroused . . . I will settle them in their homes,' declares the LORD.[7]

T So you mean that the Old Testament is all about God trying to build relationships with people and communities and connect? His aim is to get rid of sin, which means restoring good relationships, and making a real connection?

B That's not the only theme, but it's one theme. But it's not just between him and us, God wants us to love others too. He constantly tells believers not to use people for dishonest gain, to help others, and not abuse those around us. In fact, loving God but not your neighbour is not acceptable, both relationships count.

Leviticus 19:9-10

When you reap the harvest of your land, do not reap to the very edges of your field or gather the gleanings of your harvest. Do not go over your vineyard a second time or pick up the grapes that have fallen. Leave them for the poor and the foreigner. I am the LORD your God.

Leviticus 19:35-36

Do not use dishonest standards when measuring length, weight or quantity. Use honest scales and honest weights, an honest ephah and an honest hin. I am the LORD your God, who brought you out of Egypt.

Deuteronomy 24:14-15

Do not take advantage of a hired worker who is poor and needy, whether that worker is a fellow Israelite or a foreigner residing in one of your towns. Pay them their wages each day before sunset, because they are poor and are counting on it. Otherwise they may cry to the LORD against you, and you will be guilty of sin.

Amos 5:21-24

'I hate, I despise your religious festivals; your assemblies are a stench to me. Even though you bring me burnt offerings and grain offerings, I will not accept them. Though you bring choice fellowship offerings, I will have no regard for them. Away with the noise of your songs! I will not listen to the music of your harps. But let justice roll on like a river, righteousness like a never-failing stream!'

T Wow. I find this really interesting. So the Bible shows that God's aim for creation is connected loving relationships that bring love, security, self-worth, and selflessness. When these relationships fall short of a fully always-loving connection, we see alienation, loneliness, self-loathing, shame, and selfishness occurring.

This means we can say the Bible shows sin can be defined as disconnection, and the *result* is bad actions and bad stuff happening. Is that right?

B Bingo.

T So when we define sin in another way we're getting it wrong?

B No, not at all. The cross, life, and resurrection of Jesus achieved more than one thing, and sin can be defined as more than one thing. This isn't an exclusive definition. But there is a biblical theme here, meaning we can define sin as disconnection and dysfunctional relationships.

I also think this is why in the Old Testament the consequences of sin sometimes meant people were separated from their community.[8] Disconnection leads to separation and alienation.

T Is that why Jesus got so angry at the Jewish leaders sometimes? You know the ones I mean, right?

B You mean the Pharisees. But why do you say Jesus got angry at them?

T Well, the Pharisees were all about making exclusive rules, creating cliques, separating themselves from people. Whereas Jesus wanted people to treat others with love and grace, and create loving relationships. Is that right?

B That's a very good point. How Jesus treated people and saw people treated is indeed very important, and he wanted his followers to act lovingly too.

It's interesting to see what Jesus prayed just before he was arrested and killed. He prayed that future believers would be 'one'. He prayed that we would be united, and that his death would result in us connecting with God and his love. We're meant to love him back and relate well with others, and all be 'one' in him.

John 17:20-26

[Jesus said] My prayer is not for them [the twelve disciples] alone. I pray also for those who will believe in me through their message, that all of them may be one, Father, just as you are in me and I am in you. May they also be in us so that the world may believe that you have sent me. I have given them the glory that you gave me, that they may be one as we are one – I in them and you in me – so that they may be brought to complete unity. Then the world will know that you sent me and have loved them even as you have loved me. Father, I want those you have given me to be with me where I am, and to see my glory, the glory you have given me because you loved me before the creation of the world. Righteous Father, though the world does not know you, I know you, and they know that you have sent me. I have made you known to them, and will continue to make you known in order that the love you have for me may be in them and that I myself may be in them.

Or as you said, 'too much selfie isn't healthy'. Believers need to be connected with God and others in a loving and selfless way, that's what God wants.

T This is really interesting. I didn't know that the Bible saw sin like this. But how do I use this idea to talk to people about Jesus?

B In a crisis, when you call the emergency services, how do you know which one to ask for?

T Well if there's a fire, you ask for the fire service. If a crime is happening, you ask for the police. If someone is hurt, you ask for the ambulance.

B So the problem defines the solution. The people you spoke to probably don't think they've broken an ultimate law or rule, so they aren't looking for 'legal' forgiveness or a 'not guilty' verdict. But on the whole, many people feel separation, unworthiness, absence, and disappointment.

People may not use these words, but they know the feeling. Sin as disconnection means we carry a feeling similar to when we have a big argument with someone we thought loved us and wouldn't hurt us. It's like the feeling we get when we realise we've lost our close friends in the busyness of life.

Or when we pretend to be happy. Or when we get bad news, or good news, and don't know who to call or really talk to. This feeling of disconnection and wanting to overcome it. That's what people want to hear about. That's the 'forgiveness of sins' we can start with when talking to people about Jesus.

T So the reason some of my friends got annoyed and I felt bad was because I was 'calling the police when someone had broken their leg'. I should've been calling the ambulance. I was offering the wrong solution, yeah?

B That's a good way to put it. And we can all make mistakes. Part of Christianity should be about being allowed to make mistakes, asking questions and growing. And I'm sure most of them appreciated your passion for God.

T And you really think this can help me when I talk to people about God?

B Yes, because we know and experience disconnection, and they do too.

Nowadays, we all compare ourselves to friends, colleagues, famous people and pictures on social media. This generation has more access to people and images thanks to technology, more than any other in history. We now compare ourselves more and feel more insecure and unworthy than ever before.

I think people already know they aren't perfect and feel bad about their imperfections and mistakes. They don't need to be told that, they want to hear about reasons to connect instead of hiding away. People want to matter to someone, and Jesus came to bring life and show we're loved and not alone and disconnected.

John 10:10

The thief comes only to steal and kill and destroy; I have come that they may have life, and have it to the full.[9]

T But what does disconnection and relational dysfunction mean in terms of Jesus and the cross? How do I talk about sin in a way that leads people to God?

B Well, we need to take a step back and look at why Jesus was born, became human and why his life is important. Jesus' mission on Earth was to overcome sin and restore God's original intention. This means if sin is understood as broken relationships and disconnection, he was overcoming this problem and reversing the effects. Agreed?

Toby, did you get my last message?

T Yeah, sorry, they scored a last-minute goal and I had beer thrown all over me by accident. Everyone went crazy. We're just leaving now the match is over. Can I reply in a bit?

B Yeah of course, just message me when you can.

PART 2

T Hi Barney, you free to talk again?

B Good timing, Toby. I've just finished writing my preach for Sunday. Did you get back OK? Change your beer-soaked top and all that?

T Oh yeah, it's fine. We ended up bumping into some other mates on the way back and got chatting, hence the delay. They all said I was more quiet than usual. To be honest, I couldn't stop thinking about what you said.

I want to call but there are a few guys in my room now playing on my console. But I want to keep chatting.

B Feel free to keep messaging me, then. I don't have much on till later. What were you thinking about?

T Well, everything, really. I guess that I'm trying to work out, let me see if I can say this right:

if Jesus wanted to overcome sin, and sin is disconnection, then how did he overcome it?

B Let me start by making it clear that Jesus' death and resurrection are vital. However, Jesus saving us and overcoming sin started from his birth. His life and ministry are vital too. Christians sometimes forget that.

T But why is Jesus' birth and life linked to how he saves us and overcomes sin as disconnection?

B Well, put it like this, what do you need to build a good relationship?

T Trust, love, respect, acceptance, other things I can't think of right now.

B Yes, and the only way these can be truly nurtured is if there is a two-way effort. Think of your best relationships that make you feel safe and secure. Whether it's a dating relationship, friendship, etc. both participants need to show vulnerability, share intimate details, and build trust in order to create a strong, loving relationship.

T True. I guess. If someone is being fake, not being themselves, using people, or trying to be more important and control the other person, it can't work.

B Exactly. People are looking for authenticity. Something that's real. People can see if something or someone isn't being real. We have all been let down by family, friends, colleagues and wish it could be different. Deep down we all want to know someone who will love us, someone we can trust to be authentic with.

T But what does that have to do with Jesus becoming human?

B Well, the birth and life of Jesus, I would argue, is about God stepping down to build that authentic relationship. In summary, Christ came to connect. To break it down a bit more, God stepped down from heaven and became fully human for three reasons:

1: God became human because he wanted to connect with us on our level.

2: God was revealing himself, his inner intimate self, so we could connect with him.

3: Jesus was showing us how to respond to God's love for us and how to love others.

T What!? I thought Jesus came down to die on the cross?

B Jesus saves us from sin. And the incarnation, the birth of Jesus, God stepping down out of heaven in human form, is part of the solution. Not just the cross.

Take my first point, God wanted to connect with humanity on our level to create an authentic relationship. Jesus is fully human, not a fake or half human, so that God can truly experience humanity and truly connect with us and be real.

T I still don't get it. My head is spinning. You're going to have to help me out. I thought Jesus was human so he could die. Why did God need to become human in order to connect and overcome disconnection?

B Because otherwise it's not an authentic relationship. God wanted to overcome the effects of separation and broken relationships, so God himself lived like a human, grew up like a human, slept like a human, and ate like a human. Yes Jesus died on the cross, but his connection with us and the revelation of himself started at his birth.[10]

John 1:14

The Word became flesh and made his dwelling among us. We have seen his glory, the glory of the one and only Son, who came from the Father, full of grace and truth.

Philippians 2:6-8

[Jesus] who, being in very nature God, did not consider equality with God something to be used to his own advantage; rather, he made himself nothing by taking the very nature of a servant, being made in human likeness. And being found in appearance as a man, he humbled himself by becoming obedient to death – even death on a cross!

Imagine trying to get to know someone really famous. Would it be better chatting to them while reporters are constantly taking pictures and fans are screaming in a very public place, or would hanging out in a private place, just the two of you, be better?

T Oh, I think I see what you mean now. By taking away all the things that 'make them famous' and moving into a place where you are on the same level, a real relationship can be built. God became human so that we could know him on our level. Is that right?

B Yes, well put. He came to share our experience, to connect with humanity.

T But what about your second point, Jesus was revealing God's inner self. What does that mean?

B Well, Jesus is fully human and fully God at the same time. He isn't a hybrid or some strange mix.[11] A funny concept I know, but bear with me.

To fix humanity's broken relationship with God, and reverse the separation and disconnection, God had to show us who God truly is too. This is because an authentic relationship can only happen if both participants reveal who they truly are.

Importantly, only God can reveal who God is. No one can force him, otherwise he wouldn't be God. He wouldn't be the ultimate being who is uncontrolled. So only God can reveal who God is. God came to earth as Jesus, he was fully human but he was fully God too, because only God can show us what God is really like.

Hebrews 1:1-3

In the past God spoke to our ancestors through the prophets at many times and in various ways, but in these last days he has spoken to us by his Son, whom he appointed heir of all things, and through whom also he made the universe. The Son is the radiance of God's glory and the exact representation of his being ...

Colossians 1:15-20

The Son is the image of the invisible God, the firstborn over all creation. For in him all things were created ... For God was pleased to have all his fullness dwell in him, and through him to reconcile to himself all things, whether things on earth or things in heaven, by making peace through his blood, shed on the cross.

Matthew 11:27-30

'All things have been committed to me by my Father. No one knows the Son except the Father, and no one knows the Father except the Son and those to whom the Son chooses to reveal him. Come to me, all you who are weary and burdened, and I will give you rest. Take my yoke upon you and learn from me, for I am gentle and humble in heart, and you will find rest for your souls. For my yoke is easy and my burden is light.'

T But God the Father is distant, isn't he? I struggle with God as father a bit, if I'm being honest. Jesus as God the Son who is close I get, but God the Father seems distant to me.

B Remember, Christians believe in the Trinity, one God but three persons. God the Father, God the Son, and God the Holy Spirit, all distinct but one. Living in a perfect and eternal loving relationship. So Jesus is God just as truly as the Father is God.

But what's important for you to get now is that only God can reveal God, no bigger force is making him do so, otherwise he wouldn't be God.

T You've mentioned this in a preach before, I think. You said only we can reveal our true selves to people. So only Rory can reveal the inner thoughts of Rory. Only Joanne can reveal the inner hopes and feelings of Joanne. Only I can reveal who I truly am and show people my true self.

B Bingo. A key reason why God stepped out of heaven was to reveal himself, to show us who he is. He revealed his inner self so that we could truly connect with him. For true, authentic, loving relationships, we needed to know God and experience who God is. That's what Jesus did. Christ came to connect.

John 15:15

I no longer call you servants, because a servant does not know his master's business. Instead, I have called you friends, for everything that I learned from my Father I have made known to you.

John 14:9-11

Jesus answered: 'Don't you know me, Philip, even after I have been among you such a long time? Anyone who has seen me has seen the Father. How can you say, "Show us the Father"? Don't you believe that I am in the Father, and that the Father is in me? The words I say to you I do not speak on my own authority. Rather, it is the Father, living in me, who is doing his work. Believe me when I say that I am in the Father and the Father is in me; or at least believe on the evidence of the works themselves.

So going back to my analogy, it's like saying only a famous person can invite us to their home. They choose if they tell us what they're really like. We can't just storm up to their home, past the security guards, and demand that they show us what they're like can we! They come to us. God came to us.

God came down to Earth as Jesus so he could connect with us on our level, and also show us who God really is and what he is like. This two-way experience means a two-way connection can happen authentically with humanity. It's about overcoming the disconnection and truly connecting.

T Wow, this is amazing. And so I can really tell people that we have a God who is desperate to connect with us?

B Yes. It's fantastic. Sin as dysfunctional relationships brings isolation, shame and alienation but God wants to connect with us and tell us about who he really is. In the unworthiness we feel about ourselves we have a God wanting to cut through it and connect. I've explained this hundreds of time and it still gives me goose bumps.

T And you think this will connect with everyone's starting point? So I don't need to talk about 'legal' forgiveness or their 'guilt'?

B I believe this will resonate with many people's starting point, but not everyone's. If people need to know they're 'not guilty' because of Jesus, then start there. But if people need to connect, then start there. I don't want to forget about other tools in the multicoloured toolbox, but simply give people the right tool in the beginning.

We do need to learn about the other tools at some point. In fact, all Christians are learning and discovering more depth, richness and beauty when it comes to Jesus. But I'm just saying let's look at the Bible and our culture's needs, and take the most useful, relevant, and beautiful gospel truth to their starting point.

We don't need to go in with a 'legal mindset' and start with their 'guilt' necessarily.

T All of my mates in my room keep asking why I'm smiling to myself. I keep telling them it's because God is always here, even when we feel unworthy. They don't really know what to say!

B Ha ha, that's funny.

T I would have never in a million years thought that sin, Jesus' life, and him coming down to Earth could be understood like this. I assume you think the cross is still important though, right?

B Definitely. It's vital. The death and resurrection of Jesus can't be overlooked ever, and people need to accept what Jesus did on the cross and put their faith in him to receive 'forgiveness of sin'.

Only Jesus, and his birth, life, ministry, death and resurrection, can overcome all the disconnection we have caused and experienced. I'm just trying to explain why his birth and life are important. And the third point I said earlier emphasises why his ministry is vital.

T Sorry, I can't remember what you said.

B My third point was that 'Jesus was showing us how to respond to God's love for us and how to love others.'

Jesus lives out the greatest commandment and loves God with everything and loves his neighbour as himself. He teaches about, and is actively, bringing people into a relationship with him and ending the isolation and separation that people are feeling.

T Is the parable of the prodigal son about that? You know the one. The son broke his relationship with his father and community, did some unloving things and acted selfishly, but was welcomed back by his dad. Despite the shame the son felt and the damage he caused. I love that story.

B Yes, that's one way to read it. That parable is emphasising God as father, and his compassion and desire to reach people.

T And that story where Jesus meets a woman at the well who had been rejected by her community. She was alone and an outsider. But Jesus talks to her when others wouldn't, restores her to God and reconnects her to the community.

B And what about when Jesus went to the house of Zacchaeus the tax collector? The most hated profession at that time. The guy was loathed and isolated because of the choices he had made and probably because of some bad circumstances too. But Jesus builds a relationship with him and helps him to do the same with others.[12]

T Don't think I know that one. I will try to give it a read later.

B Jesus' actions and teachings show us how to love others and God. He shows us how to live a life that's full of connection. He shows us what authentic connection looks like. It doesn't mean life will be easy if we follow Jesus' example, but Jesus responded to what he saw God the Father doing. He did what the Father asked.

T But what about when Jesus was angry or spoke harshly to people? Like when he turned the tables in the temple, or did something like that, anyway?[13] Someone spoke about that at my uni church. They also said Jesus said harsh things to people who disagreed with him, like the Jewish leaders, right? Jesus was unloving sometimes?

B That's a good point, some passages do seem to teach that at first. But when you look at the overall message in the gospel, Jesus is clearly and constantly calling for deep and inner transformation. Not just external rule-following. Jesus often speaks harshly to people who think their rituals make them 'better-than-everyone-else'.

Luke 18:9-14

To some who were confident of their own righteousness and looked down on everyone else, Jesus told this parable: 'Two men went up to the temple to pray, one a Pharisee and the other a tax collector. The

Pharisee stood by himself and prayed: "God, I thank you that I am not like other people – robbers, evildoers, adulterers – or even like this tax collector. I fast twice a week and give a tenth of all I get." But the tax collector stood at a distance. He would not even look up to heaven, but beat his breast and said, "God, have mercy on me, a sinner." I tell you that this man, rather than the other, went home justified before God. For all those who exalt themselves will be humbled, and those who humble themselves will be exalted.'

It's not that Jesus is being unloving, but he has some brutal honesty for those who think external rituals are better than a deep connection and personal experience with a loving God. He wants to connect despite our faults. This connection leads to loving relationships with God and others. It offers a place to belong and overcomes sin.

Following Jesus' example may mean that we do things other people find strange, it may be hard or mean they mock us, but we need to know Jesus' example is based on love and connection. Christianity isn't about 'making my life easy' but connecting to a God who loves us and makes the first move, and promises to stick by us always.

T   So Jesus' life and ministry was showing and teaching us how live out and respond to God's love, and how we should build loving relationships with others, yeah? It's the example we follow?

B Exactly that. So you understand what I'm trying to say?

T Yeah. You're saying that Jesus wasn't just waiting to die on the cross. Rather, through his birth and life and ministry he was connecting with people. He's building relationships, reversing the effects of relational dysfunction and giving meaning to people. He's showing us what to do.

B Bingo. Like I said earlier, Jesus' birth, life and ministry can be understood as:

1: God became human because he wanted to connect with us on our level.

2: God was revealing himself, his inner intimate self, so we could connect with him.

3: Jesus was showing us how to respond to God's love for us and how to love others.

It's all summed up with the phrase: Christ came to connect.

T Just quickly, though, you talk about relationships and connection and stuff, but what about people who find it hard or strange to say they 'love' Jesus? They struggle to talk about relationships and get emotional about it? Would this not be relevant to them?

B Having an emotional attachment is part of any good relationship and good connection. But a loving relationship takes many forms; it doesn't need to only be about getting 'emotional' in the crying and showing feelings sort of way.

Put it like this: when we see our favourite sportsman or woman who we admire in action, we naturally want to find out more about them. We want to learn from them and their life and copy everything we see them doing so that our technique gets better. That's love; wanting to copy someone we admire and learn more about them.

Or how about the private in an army, who respects and obeys his commanding officer and will lay down his life to save him without hesitation? That's love, too. It's not 'showing feelings', but love can be having a deep respect and sacrificing our lives and comfort for someone else.

T That's so true.

B So it's OK to say we want to connect and form a loving relationship with Jesus, and this love is sometimes expressed by being desperate to know more about him, copy him, listen to him, respect and obey him, do what he does and give up our lives for him. It's also sometimes about getting emotional and showing feelings too.

T

This is all really amazing. Talking about sin like this could really makes Jesus seem more relevant to more people.

I mean, I know people who come from really tough families, or who have self-esteem issues, or who feel like they need to dress a certain way to fit in. People who have lots of money and look like they have it all sorted, but don't really. All these different types of people feel the effect of disconnection.

B

This connection God offers changes everything. The way we relate to others, our friendships, what we do with our weekend, the way we see ourselves, what we do with our spare time, the way we do our job, the way we think about others, what we watch on TV, how we spend our money, everything.

T

Amazing. So I can tell people that they can know Jesus today? They can get this connection now?

B

Definitely. Having an authentic relationship with someone means that we need to know facts about them, but it's also about experiencing them and hanging out together.

Imagine searching everything online that there is to know about New York. The best things to do, the best restaurants to eat at, the best places to stay. You can find out a lot. But you need to go there, stay there, experience it, to truly understand.

In the same way, God wants us to experience him and his love, and the Holy Spirit is God's presence that's still with us on Earth, so that we can know God and connect with him and have a relationship.

T

I have a lot to process. Thanks, this has really helped me! I feel excited because this stuff affects every area of my life, and not just the 'bad things' I do. Connecting is about so much more than avoiding bad stuff. It's about knowing God is there all the time, and he wants me to love him, and others, fully all the time. Amazing.

But how does the cross fit in, then? How does this understanding of sin and Jesus' life link in with the cross?

Barney, you still there?

B

Sorry, Toby. I need to go. Great question, though. The cross and resurrection are vital because without them the birth, life and ministry of

Jesus is incomplete. Jesus could just be a wise teacher. The cross changes everything, proves Jesus is more than a wise person. So we do need chat about this. When are you free?

T I should stop messaging, too. My friends keep wondering why I don't want to play on the console. I don't want to be rude. Can we chat on Tuesday, maybe? I'm free that day, no lectures.

B The life of a student, eh?! Tuesday's fine. The church is doing that meal for those who live alone in the community in the morning, so give me a call late afternoon.

T OK, chat soon, then. Thank you, Barney.

B God bless.

Current status
Just had my mind blown. God is so much bigger, and loves us so much more than I realised. Can't wait to chat to you all about him!

Author's Notes

I wrote this book because I think God is more invested in us than we could ever fully understand. I believe God wants to meet us where we're at, in our non-perfect situations, show us how much he loves us, and help us to connect in a truly life-changing way.

As you read my notes about the previous chapter, please think about what stood out to you in the chats between Barney and Toby, and how you could potentially put some of this into action.

Sin as Disconnection

Key Takeaways

- Sin's effects, and the very definition of sin, can be understood in more than one way in the Bible.

- One definition is: disconnection/dysfunctional relationships.

- Many people in our culture, in and outside of the church, want to overcome disconnection, which brings things like shame, isolation, and feeling unworthy. They want to find a way to connect, and find a place where they're always accepted and belong, no matter what.

Real Life Stories

As I was writing this book, I was chatting to a friend who said a guy she met had become a Christian and started going to church about five months prior. She said this guy was talking about how had found a real joy since knowing Jesus. Before my friend could say anything in reply, he said to her, 'But I'm trying to stop swearing, and I'm trying to stop spending money on things I don't need, and I'm trying to stop this, and I'm trying to stop that . . . ' The list went on and on.

My friend said to me, 'It didn't sound very joyful. It sounded like a prison sentence. Like he was scared if he got anything wrong he would be kicked out of the club.' She was genuinely concerned that this new Christian was reducing his understanding of Jesus and his cross to rules he had broken, but she found it hard to explain to him why the cross should mean so much more.

I also remember going to a talk when I was a fairly new Christian, and starting to mentor and disciple younger people myself. The speaker said he did a lot of mentoring in his church. He then said, 'I hate it when mentoring is reduced to "What have you done wrong this week?" As if God is just concerned with what mistakes we've made. God's impact and vision for our lives is bigger. His purpose for our lives is so much more than "Stop doing that!" He wants us to know him and hang out with him and use us to change lives.'

I wanted to share these stories with you because they show that we can unintentionally reduce sin and the cross to a list of 'do not's'. Now obviously, there are things we need to stop doing. However, we can focus on these things so much that we can unintentionally forget Jesus also established new realities on the cross, like a fully connected, always there, unconditional loving relationship with himself.

Real Life Application

When people in the church ask me about how these new realities can impact their daily life and relationships with God and others, I get them to think about how they deal with sin/disconnection. We shouldn't just think about how we avoid it, but how we can *replace* it with habits and actions that bring connection and fully loving relationships.

For example, I won't just stop gossiping, I'll start saying encouraging things about people. I won't just stop using God's name in vain, I'll start praying more.

Some good questions to ask are:

- Does this thought, word or action create connections?

- Is what I'm doing making my relationship/connection with God and others stronger or weaker?

I also hope you are empowered to talk about your faith (or think about it for the first time) in a way that emphasises God can meet and relate to us in a place of broken relationships, shame and unworthiness. He can overcome our disconnection.

Key Bible Verses

Genesis 2:25; 3:7-10; Revelation 21:1-4; Mark 12:28-31; 2 Corinthians 5:14-15; John 15:14-17; 17:20-26.

Further Reading

Blocher, H.A.G., 'Sin', in Alexander, T.D., and Rosner, B.S. (eds.), *New Dictionary of Biblical Theology*, Leicester: IVP, 2006, 781-788.

Lodahl, M., 'Sin In Relational Perspective' in Montgomery, B., Oord, T.J., and Winslow, K. (eds.), *Relational Theology: A Contemporary Introduction,* Eugene, OR: Wipf & Stock, 2012, 37-39.

Peterson, B.D., 'Worship as Relational Renewal and Redemption of the World', in Montgomery, B., Oord, T.J., and Winslow, K. (eds.), *Relational Theology: A Contemporary Introduction*, Eugene, OR: Wipf & Stock, 2012, 76-79.

Pugh, B., *Atonement Theories: A Way Through the Maze*, Eugene, OR: Cascade, 2014.

Christ Came to Connect

Key Takeaways

- Jesus didn't just come to Earth to die on the cross. His birth, life and ministry play a key role in saving us and overcoming sin.

- God became human because he wanted to connect with us on our level.

- God was revealing himself, his inner intimate self, so we could connect with him.

- Jesus was showing us how to respond to God's love for us and how to love others.

Real Life Stories

This powerful story was shared at my church by someone who had been volunteering at a Christian festival the previous summer:

I was helping at a Christian camp as a youth worker. One evening service when most people were worshipping, a young lad came to ask me for prayer. He was wearing a jumper even though it was really hot and we were all in T-shirts. He said he had a really bad skin condition and it was worse on his arms. He didn't want people to see it so he always wore long sleeves. He asked me to pray for God to heal him.

As a team, we had prayed for a few other people during the week and seen some amazing healings. So me and this lad started praying about his skin. But nothing changed. We kept praying for ages. Nothing changed. It was really disappointing, and even though we could sense God's presence, his skin wasn't changing.

I suddenly felt prompted to tell him that God really loves him, that God really cares for him, that God is with him and that God understands. These words seemed to really impact him.

We were praying for a bit longer then we stopped. The young lad was quiet for a bit, then he took his jumper off, ran to the front of the room and started singing and worshipping with everyone else. He was there with his hands raised and jumper off, everyone could see his arms and he was singing God's praises.

It reminded me that sometimes God heals, sometimes he doesn't. I don't get it, I don't understand. But God will always be with us.

For me, this story highlights two important points. Firstly, life is rubbish sometimes. Sometimes we're struggling not because of the bad things we've done, but because of the bad things being done to us. We feel isolated, alone, unsure, embarrassed. And things won't always turn out how we would like.

However, God is with us no matter what. He loves us and will always be there. He sees our situation, good and bad, and sticks around anyway. He can connect with us and be there, even when we're struggling to even like ourselves.

Real Life Application

I used to always sit there in church and think everyone had it sorted but me. God loved them but not me because of what I did last week, month, year or whatever. I would place barriers between me and God/other people, because I was too scared to let them see the real me. I was just letting everyone down and feeling fake, distant and alone.

I now know that God wanting a relationship isn't just a by-product of Jesus' life and death, it's at the very heart of his life and death when we emphasise biblical truths (without discounting others). God is longing to connect, he wants to meet us in our angst, our fear and in our longing to be real and honest, and he builds authentic relationships with us.

We need to remember that God is interested in the real us and is always there. As we emphasise the biblical theme of connection, we can make Jesus even more attractive to our society and our friends, and meet them at their starting point of disconnection.

Some questions worth thinking about are:

- How do I make sure I run towards God, and not away from him, when I feel disconnection?

- What can I do to make sure I'm regularly and intentionally connecting with God? E.g. reading my Bible, painting, singing, serving, dancing, taking communion, listening to talks, hanging out as a Christian community, or anything that allows me to be real, more honest and grow our relationship.

Key Bible Verses

John 1:14, 15:15; 17:25-26; Colossians 1:15-20; Hebrews 1:1-3; Jeremiah 31:31-34.

Further Reading

Smail, T., *Like Father, Like Son: The Trinity Imaged in Our Humanity*, Milton Keynes: Paternoster, 2005.

Sweet, J., 'Docetism: Is Jesus Christ really human or did he just appear to be so?', in

Quash, B., and Ward, M. (eds.), *Heresies and How to Avoid Them: Why it Matters What Christians Believe,* London: SPCK, 2007, 24-31.

Thompson, M.B., 'Arianism: Is Jesus Christ divine and eternal or was he created?', in Quash, B., and Ward, M. (eds.), *Heresies and How to Avoid Them*, 15-23.

Tomlin, G., *The Widening Circle: Priesthood as God's Way of Blessing the World*, London: SPCK, 2014.

Chapter 2

'Am I loved?'

The cross and resurrection restores relationships

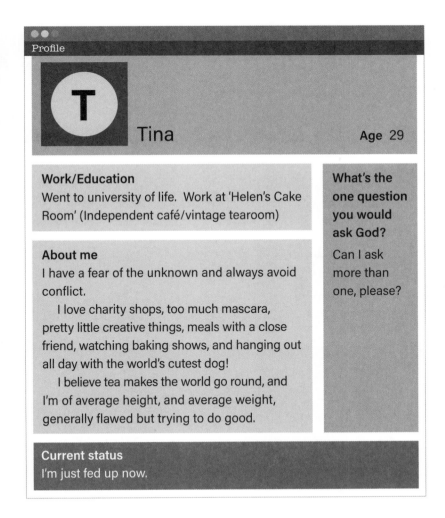

Profile

T

Tina   Age 29

Work/Education
Went to university of life. Work at 'Helen's Cake Room' (Independent café/vintage tearoom)

About me
I have a fear of the unknown and always avoid conflict.
    I love charity shops, too much mascara, pretty little creative things, meals with a close friend, watching baking shows, and hanging out all day with the world's cutest dog!
    I believe tea makes the world go round, and I'm of average height, and average weight, generally flawed but trying to do good.

What's the one question you would ask God?
Can I ask more than one, please?

Current status
I'm just fed up now.

PART 1

T I'm so sorry, Barney. I can't make it to you this afternoon now. Something has come up at work, again! So sorry. I'll explain later. Sorry.

B Don't worry, Tina. I haven't left the office yet. We can rearrange. When are you next free?

T Hi. Sorry for not responding yesterday. And for cancelling at the last second. My colleague didn't turn up for work so my boss said I had to cover. I said I had plans but she said she did too and I had to stay. I just couldn't say no to her. I was so upset and taking it out on the new guy, and most of my baking was going wrong that day too.

It was all so stressful. I got home and shut myself away and binge-watched my new favourite series. Sorry, I should've texted yesterday to explain. I just thought you might be mad. Sorry.

B Hello. Don't worry about it. I know you're struggling at work. I was looking forward to meeting up and discussing the questions you asked me about Jesus and the gospel. But I was able to meet with someone else from church instead, so don't worry. No harm done. Do you want to rearrange?

T I'll let you know when I know my shifts. I'm going in later. Just trying to relax at the moment.

B OK. I'll pray for your work situation, and that you'll be able to sort stuff out with your boss and the colleagues you're struggling with.

T Yeah, maybe I will too. It's just hard sometimes.

B What do you mean?

T Well, I just mean, I have prayed but, oh never mind. It's just hard, and I'm tired. I'm fed up. I just need some time.

B Are you upset because you've been praying and nothing's changing?

Tina?

T Kind of, yeah. But you can pray for me, though.

B I know it's hard sometimes, but God is listening and is with you. I'm sure of it. Please don't feel like he isn't. He loves you and cares for you.

T What's the point in praying, though, when nothing's happening?! It's so frustrating. I just can't be bothered sometimes. Maybe he can't hear me.

B Come on, Tina, you know that God isn't a genie or Santa Claus, or an aid from our self-help programme. He doesn't promise us an easy, hassle-free life, but he does promise to always be there no matter what. To be fully connected and to never leave us.

---

1 John 4:13-16

This is how we know that we live in him and he in us: he has given us of his Spirit. And we have seen and testify that the Father has sent his Son to be the Saviour of the world. If anyone acknowledges that Jesus is the Son of God, God lives in them and they in God. And so we know and rely on the love God has for us. God is love. Whoever lives in love lives in God, and God in them.

Matthew 28:18-20

Then Jesus came to them and said, 'All authority in heaven and on earth has been given to me. Therefore go and make disciples of all nations, baptising them in the name of the Father and of the Son and of the Holy Spirit, and teaching them to obey everything I have commanded you. And surely I am with you always, to the very end of the age.'

Psalm 23:4

Even though I walk through the darkest valley, I will fear no evil, for you are with me; your rod and your staff, they comfort me.

God is with you in the struggle with your boss and colleagues, even if you can't always tell. He loves you and is involved. He is listening.

T Well, it doesn't feel like it! They all just make me feel so unconfident and isolated. I'm just fed up.

You say these things, but how can I be sure God is with me all the time? How do I really know he loves me?

B Because of the cross, because of Jesus' death and resurrection.

T Well, maybe I'm still not good enough. When I do something I know I shouldn't, or think something bad about someone at work, maybe God then doesn't love me as much. Or maybe he can't hear me praying for some reason. I just can't see anything changing.

B I can tell you're feel really frustrated. And that's OK. You're questioning if God's love for you is real, and if he's really always there and connected. And it's OK to be honest and ask these questions. Can I call to chat about this?

T I would prefer to just text. I can't face talking to anyone at the moment. Besides, I feel bad asking these questions. Texting makes it easier.

B Well, don't feel bad. I'm working from home today and doing some boring admin jobs. All interruptions are very welcome! Did you get a chance to reflect and think about what we discussed the last time we met up?

T Yeah. And, well, I guess I got what you said about sin. How it can be defined as disconnection and broken relationships. I get why Jesus became human and came to Earth. But I didn't quite understand the cross and resurrection bit. I still struggle with it and have so many questions.

I mean, how does someone dying 2,000 years ago help me at work? Help me know I'm loved? I just want to hide away sometimes.

B I understand. You're not the only one who thinks like that, you know. Lots of people struggle with Jesus' death. We all have questions, I still do.

T Really? But you work for the church. Do you really have questions as well?

B Yeah, of course. We all have bits about God and the Bible that we think are strange, harsh or odd. I believe we should ask those questions if we want to take our relationship with God seriously. That's what I think, anyway.

T Having come back to God and church recently, I feel like I shouldn't ask these sorts of things sometimes. We're told to have faith when we don't understand and realise that God is above our understanding. And I do want more faith, but these questions won't leave me.

B Well, I think God wants us to ask questions and think for ourselves. But I want to stress that the cross changes everything. It changes disconnection into connection, and allows us to relate fully to God. It means God is always close to you and with you in the situations you face. It really does answer your problems and needs.

T But how! How does it help me now? How do I know God is close? How do I know he still loves me, no matter what? It just doesn't all fit in my mind.

Sometimes at church I feel like we're made to treat Jesus like a 'magician'. We see him die, then he reappears, and we clap. We're meant to believe it's real and not ask how it's done. But I just need to ask someone.

Sorry, Barney, I hope you don't mind me saying that. I do feel bad. Faith is important and I know I won't grasp it all, but I want to know I'm giving my life to something that matters. Sorry. Maybe these questions are why God doesn't love me.

B Let me make it clear, God loves you. That's the beginning and conclusion to all of this. He sees all of these questions you ask and feel bad about. He sees your work situation and all those times when you think you're not good enough. He loves you. Everything I'm about to say starts and ends with divine, limitless, uncontrollable love.

He loves you when you feel bad about yourself, he loves you when you reject him, ignore him, walk away from him or ask questions. He loves you and wants a relationship. That's the foundation and where it all begins.

T But if overcoming sin, disconnection, bad relationships or whatever is the focus of the cross, then sin is the motivation, right? Sin would come before love?

B The problem is the sin, but the motivation is love. Disconnection is the problem, but wanting to connect and form loving relationships is the motivation. That's why Jesus was born and why Jesus died on the cross.

Romans 5:8
But God demonstrates his own love for us in this: while we were still sinners, Christ died for us.

John 3:16-17
For God so loved the world that he gave his one and only Son, that whoever believes in him shall not perish but have eternal life. For God

did not send his Son into the world to condemn the world, but to save the world through him.

Imagine if someone randomly buys you a gift because you're feeling down or upset. Assuming they genuinely and wholeheartedly did it without wanting anything in return, their motivation is love. They want to help you, to connect, maybe. You feeling hurt and upset is the problem, but the motivation is love.

T Maybe. I just think it's too good to be true. Why would they want to get *me* a gift? Can there really be a God who loves me despite all of the relational dysfunction? In all of the disconnection? In all of my isolation and shame? I just don't know.

1 John 4:10
This is love: not that we loved God, but that he loved us and sent his Son as an atoning sacrifice for our sins.

B So many people think, 'God loves other people, but not *me*. If you knew the real me, what I've done or said, you would realise it.' Or they think God is hateful and distant and angry all the time. But God's motivation is love. No one forced him to save us. He wanted to have a relationship.

So often we compare ourselves to other people, not living up to their standards, not being as happy as people on social media, not being as rich as others. We feel shame, disconnection, we try to hide our true selves. It's like we want to wear a mask or be someone else, because we think that might make us lovable.

T Do other people really feel like this too?

B Yes, they really do! We've all felt like this. Whether it's because of a broken family, losing touch with friends and feeling alone, a failed romantic relationship, an unfulfilling career. We feel disconnected and want to change it, but we feel like no one could be that loving to 'me'.

T Well, I know that I'm not perfect, but I just don't want life to be like this. Feeling that I don't fit in. Feeling like I don't belong. Like something is missing.

B Exactly. We all experience the effects and we all cause the effects of relational dysfunction. Ultimately, we don't want life to be like this. We want our lives to matter. We want to know we're loved for who we are and build good relationships that make us feel safe and secure.

Amazingly, the cross starts with God's love for us.

T I bet you wished I didn't ask all these questions!

B No, I'm glad you asked, don't feel bad. Yes, we've all sinned, related and been related to unloving, which causes shame and separation. But we can connect to God and others because of the cross and experience real change. The cross isn't an optional extra, though, but an offer that can really answer our needs. If we let it.

T I see what you mean. We wouldn't even be talking about the cross, and how to connect with God, unless he made it all happen. I guess he wouldn't go through that unless he cared.

B Jesus is love in person. The cross brings forgiveness of sins and loving relationships. Love can't be lower than first place.

T I wish accepting love and loving others was easier sometimes. I just find it hard because people have hurt me.

B It is hard. We can all find it hard. We need to be real and honest about that. But that's why forgiveness is so important. It isn't easy and is often a long process, and forgiveness doesn't mean ignoring the pain or pretending it doesn't matter. But forgiving others, creating a fresh start, is part of building loving relationships.

T I still find it hard. But I know we all make mistakes.

B We do. The soup kitchen volunteer may still gossip about their friends. The colleague who always makes the newbie feel welcome may still tell lots of lies. Or those who refuse to help someone in need because they're still angry at them. We feel the pain when someone is being selfish and relating unlovingly, but we do it, too.

No one is fully loving and fully perfect. We unfortunately hurt others, in big ways and small ways. We also hurt God. Restoring connection and loving relationships the way God wants us to involves forgiving each other and ourselves, accepting forgiveness, and accepting the cross.

T But why did Jesus have to die for God to forgive us? Why did a loving God kill his son? Why couldn't an all-powerful God just connect with us and just forgive our dysfunctional relationships? I don't get it.

B Firstly, we must remember Jesus was more than 30 years old when he died. He *willingly* went to the cross. He wanted to do it because of the result it would bring.[1] That doesn't mean it was easy or fun, but he did choose it as an adult.

John 15:13

[Jesus said] Greater love has no one than this: to lay down one's life for one's friends.

Also, Jesus is God, he is part of the Trinity; God the Father, God the Son and God the Holy Spirit, all distinct, but all one God. So when Jesus suffered, God was choosing to suffer *as* a human, in our humanity, in the same way we do. God didn't just kill his unwilling child, God paid the price himself.[2] This act deals with sin.

T OK, but why did Jesus have to die? Why couldn't God just connect with us?

B Well, we know that if someone has done something wrong to us and hurt us but we choose to forgive them, and build a good relationship instead of weakening it, that choice costs us something. We can choose to absorb the negative effects rather than pass them on. But it costs us something. It's never free. It's never easy.

T What do you mean?

B For example, if someone breaks your expensive TV and you tell them not to worry about it, that isn't easy. You have absorbed and taken on the financial cost and hassle instead of passing it on to them. It costs you something.

If a friend or family member really lets us down, we can choose to forgive and not let it affect the relationship. But the pain is still there. The hurt is still there. We can still get upset. But we choose to absorb it, suffer it, instead of hurting them back. That isn't easy, it costs us something. Forgiveness and connection is never free.[3]

T I guess when you put it like that it makes sense. I'm always amazed at families on TV who come out after their relative has been murdered and say they forgive the person who did it.

B That wasn't easy for them. They're obviously hurting. Our experience of relationships sadly shows us that we hurt people and get hurt. But we can choose to connect rather than disconnect and hold a grudge. But no one 'just' forgives, or builds and restores a loving relationship easily. There's a cost.

T OK. So the motivation of the cross is God's love, but there's a price to restoring a fully connected loving relationship, to bringing forgiveness, and the cross is paying that price. Right?

B Correct.

T But you still haven't told me why Jesus had to die. Why was the cost death? And why does Jesus' death mean that this loving God is with me always and always connected?

B Let's break down your questions a bit. There is a reason why it was Jesus, and not just a prophet, or a random believer.

Jesus came down and lived like a human on Earth. One reason for this is because he showed humanity how to connect to God and others. He was responding to God's love as a human and he always lived out the greatest commandment, meaning Jesus loved God and his neighbour all the time.

This is important because it means he never sinned. He was never unloving. He lived an authentic, fully-connected human life. His actions and attitudes never hurt others or God. He was never selfish because he was always connected. He had no disconnection. He had no sin in him.

---

1 Peter 2:21-22

To this you were called, because Christ suffered for you, leaving you an example, that you should follow in his steps. 'He committed no sin, and no deceit was found in his mouth.'

Hebrews 4:15

For we do not have a high priest who is unable to feel sympathy for our weaknesses, but we have one who has been tempted in every way, just as we are – yet he did not sin.

T Why does that matter?

B Because Jesus is therefore unique. He was the first and only human to never sin, meaning his death is also unique. He is dying as the human who never sinned, and this uniqueness ultimately means he can truly pay the cost of forgiveness, by surrendering his perfect life through his death.

T Sorry, but you still haven't really answered me. Why death? Even if it was unique, why did this sinless human have to die on the cross? Why does it matter to me when I go into work? I still don't get it!

B Like I've said many times, I truly believe Jesus achieved many things on the cross. But when disconnection is the problem and the context of sin, then the biblical truth that is important to emphasise is: On the cross there was a 'sacrifice' and a 'ransom' paid.

T I've heard those words said before, but I'm not fully sure what they mean.

B If we lived 2,000 years ago, these words would have been very common. When the Bible was written, these concepts were part of the culture. People made daily sacrifices and saw ransoms being paid. Which is why we need to take some time to understand how the gospel writers used these words 2,000 years ago.

Take sacrifice – put simply, the word sacrifice means: something of value dies so that something else lives.

T Sacrifice is something God commanded, right? It was something he wanted his people to do?

B Yes, but it's something lots of cultures and religions have done since the dawn of time, really. It's not just unique to Christianity or Judaism. In fact, people in the Bible made sacrifices to God before he commanded them to, like when Noah sacrificed animals after he left the ark; Cain and Abel made sacrifices too.[4]

T So what was the point of making sacrifices, what happened as a result?

B Well, the Bible has lots of stories involving sacrifices. And what we see is that the sacrifice clearly maintains the relationship between God and his people before Jesus dies. We read that it brings 'forgiveness of sins' and wipes the slate clean, it brings peace and well-being, and the sacrifice works because it pleases God.[5]

Leviticus 14:19-20

Then the priest is to sacrifice the sin offering and make atonement for the one to be cleansed from their uncleanness. After that, the priest shall slaughter the burnt offering and offer it on the altar, together with the grain offering, and make atonement for them, and they will be clean.

T So what you're saying is that the sacrifice changes something. It does something. It restores our relationship with God and reverses the damage and brings forgiveness. By making a 'sacrifice', everything is OK?

B Well, yes and no. The sacrifices are important and God graciously, out of love, established them so that people could connect and reconnect to him. But he wasn't bound by them. If people did them for show, or weren't loving their neighbour whilst doing it, the sacrifice meant nothing to God.[6]

Proverbs 21:3

To do what is right and just is more acceptable to the LORD than sacrifice.

T That makes sense if it's about a relationship and connecting and not just ticking a box. But how did the sacrifices work, exactly?

B The Bible makes it clear that the sacrifices brought people back into a relationship with God, especially on the 'Day of Atonement'. This was when the people of God came together and 'placed' their sin on the scapegoat and it took away their sin. Then the scapegoat was sent into the wilderness to die as a sacrifice.[7]

I know it's not exactly animal friendly, but in the sacrificial system the people were able to take all their sin, all the relational dysfunction they caused and experienced, all the things that separated them from God and others, and deal with it.

115

This physical death affected the non-physical unseen things, like relationships.

T Scapegoat? I always thought it was a lamb.

B Lambs play a key role too. For example, God commanded that two lambs were sacrificed every day so that he could daily meet and connect to his people. The blood of the Passover lamb saved God's people from disaster when they were slaves in Egypt.[8]

T But how exactly does sacrifice change the unseen things?

B Because the life of the animal was surrendered. Essentially, sin leads to 'death', so sin needs to be dealt with so that 'life' is restored. The life of the animal was surrendered to cover up the sin, meaning death was dealt with, and life was restored to the people. In other words, disconnection was replaced with connection.

The life was represented by the blood, so the blood was spilt to make the sacrifice and surrender the life of the animal in order to change things.[9]

Leviticus 17:11

For the life of a creature is in the blood, and I have given it to you to make atonement for yourselves on the altar; it is the blood that makes atonement for one's life.

T Let me see if I get it. What you're saying is that sacrifices were commanded by God. They allowed people to connect with him by dealing with sin, the barriers and distorted relationship effects. The blood of the animal changed things. It brought 'life', by which you mean it brings unseen things like connection.

So when people made sacrifices to God, it reversed the effects of sin and made it all OK?

B Yes, but the sacrifices aren't necessarily *to God*. The Bible never says all sacrifices, or the sacrifice Jesus made on the cross, was *to God*. It was a sacrifice *for us*, and this may be the best way to understand it.

T Surely it was a sacrifice to God. What do you mean *for* us?

B Think about this: when a solder dies in battle, let's say he sacrifices his life by diving on a grenade to save his comrades, he didn't make a sacrifice *to* the enemy. He made a sacrifice *for* his comrades, *for* the country he's fighting to protect.

Or imagine the single parent who has two jobs and sacrifices their time, energy and own meals to feed and care for their kids. The sacrifices are *for* the kids. Not to the bosses, or the taxman, or the companies they pay their bills to.

T I always thought Jesus made a sacrifice to God on the cross, or to the devil. That's what I heard a lot when I was growing up. But you're saying the Bible never says that?

B Not explicitly, or at least consistently.[10] What we do know is that the biblical authors understood the cross as a sacrifice. In the Bible it's clear that sacrifices restore people's relationship with God first, and then with others, too.

T So why don't we make sacrifices anymore?

B Because Jesus' sacrifice is enough. Jesus loved God and his neighbour fully all the time. He then surrendered his perfect, sinless, unique life, and his unique death was enough to cover up and deal with all sin, past, present and future, for good.

T How do you know that?

B Because the Bible makes it clear that Jesus is the perfect lamb. He is the sacrifice that can change things forever. Jesus' blood has been spilt, his blood represented his perfect life, which can cover up the sin and disconnect and restore life and connection forever.

John 1:29

The next day John saw Jesus coming towards him and said, 'Look, the Lamb of God, who takes away the sin of the world!'

Hebrews 9:22-28

In fact, the law requires that nearly everything be cleansed with blood, and without the shedding of blood there is no forgiveness . . . But [Jesus] has appeared once for all at the culmination of the ages to do away with sin by the sacrifice of himself . . . so Christ was sacrificed once to take away the sins of many . . .

Hebrews 10:10-14

And by that will, we have been made holy through the sacrifice of the body of Jesus Christ once for all . . . But when this priest had offered for all time one sacrifice for sins, he sat down at the right hand of God . . . For by one sacrifice he has made perfect for ever those who are being made holy.

Something of value died so that something else lives.

T I've never heard the cross explained like this before. It's so helpful. It clearly isn't a random thing. It means something. It's about God's love for us and God paying the price to change things. I feel a bit more hopeful, even if I'm a bit confused, too!

B On the cross, Jesus died, and his sacrifice, his blood, was *for* us. It covers up and changes all of the relational dysfunction. The Bible says the sacrifice deals with sin, and all the shame, isolation, and other things that go with it. Jesus, the perfect, sinless human could, and did, make the perfect and ultimate transforming sacrifice.

His death restored relationships so much that the connection cannot be lost despite what we've done or will do. The change has happened, and if we accept Jesus and his sacrifice, we gain the benefits.

T I think I get that, kind of, anyway. I need to think of a picture to try to get it fully though. You know how my brain works.

B Well, imagine our relationship with God is like an old road: it has chips in it, potholes and bits missing. Imagine the road is so bad that riding your bike or car over it is dangerous. That's what sin does. It leaves our relationship with God ruined. We feel bad, shameful, unworthy, left wondering if anyone can help us.

But when this road gets tarmac put on it, all the holes, all the chips and all the problems are covered over *and* filled in. The road is made new and safe. The cross is like that. The sacrifice, the blood of Jesus, covers and restore the holes, the chips, the separation, the isolation. This brings a good road and a good relationship with God.

The disconnection is dealt with. The potholes are fixed and restored and the effect is permanent. Nothing can take away our connection with God.

T What is it that person said last Sunday when they were preaching? It's like when snow falls on a rubbish tip. Snow covers it up and makes it look clean.

B Yes, but snow only covers over the rubbish. Tarmac will cover over a pothole *and* fill it in and reverse the problem. It fully deals with it. Jesus' sacrifice means we can connect to God. Jesus has sorted the problem if we trust him. We can now relate to him and trust that this relationship is strong and safe. He will never walk away.

T But the tarmac isn't permanent.

B Very true, which is where the analogy breaks down. But you get the point, I'm sure. The sacrifice isn't to God to change his mind. It's for us. To make sure we can connect to God and have a loving relationship. Jesus made the sacrifice to overcome sin, and deal with the problem of disconnection permanently.

Romans 5:17-19

For if, by the trespass of the one man, death reigned through that one man, how much more will those who receive God's abundant provision of grace and of the gift of righteousness reign in life through the one man, Jesus Christ! Consequently, just as one trespass resulted in condemnation for all people, so also one righteous act resulted in justification and life for all people. For just as through the disobedience of the one man the many were made sinners, so also through the obedience of the one man the many will be made righteous.

Hebrews 9:11-14

[Jesus] did not enter by means of the blood of goats and calves; but he entered the Most Holy Place once for all by his own blood, so obtaining eternal redemption. The blood of goats and bulls and the ashes of a heifer sprinkled on those who are ceremonially unclean sanctify them so that they are outwardly clean. How much more, then, will the blood of Christ, who through the eternal Spirit offered himself unblemished to God, cleanse our consciences from acts that lead to death, so that we may serve the living God!

T I don't really like the idea of death, though. And blood freaks me out.

B Me too, but in modern cultures where many people, at least in urban contexts, don't do any farming and food comes wrapped in neat packages, we forget that something needs to die for something else to live. One animal dies, so that another one can eat. A plant dies and fertilises the ground for the next plant.

T That is a bit of a random point, why does that matter?

B There is a rhythm to creation. Ask any scientist. Something dies and something else lives. Cells in our bodies die so that new ones can form and we can keep going. A sacrifice is made and death brings life. An animal dies and is sacrificed so that the people of God can live. The authors of the Bible understood sacrifice like this.

John 12:24

Very truly I tell you, unless a grain of wheat falls to the ground and dies, it remains only a single seed. But if it dies, it produces many seeds.

The cost of wiping the slate clean and God forgiving our sins was death, because death brings life. The perfect human died on the cross, and absorbed the cost of forgiveness to deal with the damage done by sin and disconnection. His perfect life was surrendered and replaces our disconnection with a permanent connection.

T But what does this new connection, this new life, look like for us now? How can I know God loves me and is with me always?

B Well, this is where the idea of ransom becomes important. Like I said, the cross is a sacrifice, but also a ransom (and other things too). Interesting fact: ransom is the only concept Jesus used to describe his own death. He knew it was coming,[11] but 'ransom' is the only word he himself used to explain why he would die.

Matthew 20:28
[Jesus said] Just as the Son of Man did not come to be served, but to serve, and to give his life as a ransom for many.

T This word always confused me. Am I right in saying it means when someone pays a price to let someone else go free? Sorry if that's wrong.

B Yes, essentially. A price is paid, often a very big one, and consequently someone or a group of people are set free and/or 'redeemed'. Redeemed basically means being made right again. Or that something is being restored to what it should be, that kind of idea.

The Bible, like with sacrifice, doesn't make it clear who the ransom is paid to, but the biblical writers clearly see the cross as a ransom. As a result, we are redeemed and 'restored to what we should be' because of it.

T And you're saying the word 'ransom' was common when the Bible was written?

B Oh yeah. For example, in the Bible someone could pay a ransom price and redeem a slave or someone who has been condemned to die. Or even a property they once owned. God himself redeemed the Israelites and set them free from slavery in Egypt, because God has always been in the business of freeing people.[12]

T Argh, I've just seen the time! I need to start getting ready and go to work. You are distracting me too much! But very quickly, what was the ransom price Jesus paid?

B Jesus paid with his own life. He himself was the ransom price. His death was the price that was paid so that 'many' and all people could benefit and go free.

1 Timothy 2:6

[Jesus] gave himself as a ransom for all people. This has now been witnessed to at the proper time.

Hebrews 9:15

For this reason Christ is the mediator of a new covenant, that those who are called may receive the promised eternal inheritance – now that he has died as a ransom to set them free from the sins committed under the first covenant.

1 Corinthians 6:19-20

Do you not know that your bodies are temples of the Holy Spirit, who is in you, whom you have received from God? You are not your own; you were bought at a price. Therefore honour God with your bodies.

Imagine waking up one day and feeling alone, ashamed and separated. Then across the road you see a loving family. You see happy people and long to join in and feel loved. But when you go up to the house you cannot go in because all that disconnection and those broken relationships has marked you. You don't feel worthy.

Your view of yourself stops you. You're scared, isolated, worried. But then someone comes out of the house and says you can take his place. He says he's always known you and always wanted you to join in. He thinks you're good enough. He says take his place inside the house and join the family. He has sorted it.

T This is a really nice picture, but why would I get to take their place in the house?

B Because Jesus' ransom means we go free *and* he also switched places with us. This means we can now stand where he stands with his status as a loved child of God.[13] We can be as close to God the Father as Jesus, the sinless human, was. We change places and get his status. We get to join God's loving family.

Without the cross we are trapped in the place of disconnect, and are causing and affected by dysfunctional relationships. Sin is holding us back from having the life we crave. We don't want life to be like it is. We want to connect, feel safe enough to be the real us, be loved and accepted, but we can't change this on our own.

T Whereas Jesus lived a life that was loving towards God and his neighbour. Fully connected to God the Father and his neighbour. So he can bring about the change through his death on the cross. Right?

B Correct. He had freedom and connection, he was in the family, his life was fulfilling and authentic. The perfect human, who didn't need saving, swapped places and stood in our place.

Because of his death, we can now go free and also enjoy the benefits of his status and connection. His death paid the ransom price we couldn't pay, so his cross restores us to what we should be. Namely, experiencing a fully connected relationship with God.

T Barney, I'm rushing around trying to get ready, I really do need to go soon. But I never knew ransom meant that.

B Before you go, let me say again: love is the motivation. God wants to overcome sin, restore relationships and connect, but it costs something. Jesus' life was sinless and therefore unique, meaning his death is unique too.

His death is a sacrifice, which means it's for us, covers us and deals with sin and brings permanent change. His death is a ransom, too, a payment and a swap, so we go free and stand in his place of connection. We get to fully connect to God's love and have a close relationship with him and others. It's amazing really.

T I have so many more questions, but I really need to go now, sorry. Can we chat more later? I need to think about all of this. I still need to know how this impacts my daily life, affects me at work, and brings change.

B I know. I'm getting to that point though, I promise! When do you finish work? There is a big group of us going out later for a drink. If you come we can finish talking about this then?

T OK, I will text you after work. Thanks for making me feel a bit better. I'm still dreading work but I can see the cross isn't just random or senseless. God really did something significant.

B He definitely did. I will be praying for you. See you later. I'll text you about times and location.

PART 2

T Hi, Barney, I've just finished my shift and got back home. I'm so shattered. Do you mind if I don't come out with you and the gang? Sorry, I know I'm being boring but I just need to rest a bit.

B Hello. No worries. I'm about to eat my dinner, then I'll go afterwards. There's a good number of us going if you do change your mind. How was work?

T It was OK, thanks. Not perfect but better. It's far from perfect, in fact, but it was better. I felt better. It helped that I was thinking about all of this stuff, too. I still have so many questions. Can I text you them, please?

B Sure, do you want to call? Would that be easier?

T Let's text for now, thanks.

B OK, fire away, then.

T So we talked about why God did it and why Jesus had to die, and that sacrifice and ransom changes things, but how does it bring the connection you always talk about? I really need to understand why this means God is with me, and loves me in my daily life and struggles, no matter what. And what that reality looks like.

I guess I'm trying to figure how the effects of the cross affect us now, today, and get it all clear in my head.

B Well, if we view sin as dysfunctional relationships and disconnection, then the cross is establishing good, loving relationships. It overcomes the problem of sin by bringing connection. Put simply, the cross and resurrection restores relationships. But if we expanded on this point, I would say:

1: It allows us to have the status and fully loving relationship Jesus had with God, we are fully connected with him. He sees our true selves and will never leave us.

2: Past and future disconnection, relational dysfunction and its effects which separate us have been dealt with and overcome permanently. These things don't define us or create separation now, they are reversed. Connection is here to stay.

3: We know we're loved, we belong and are wanted because we are brought into God's loving family, with loving brothers and sisters and a loving father.

T What does all of this mean, exactly?

B I know you're very visual, so let me put it like this. The cross is a bit like running home to a relative that will make you feel loved and wanted, or to the friend that makes us feel better and comforted. All our problems don't necessarily disappear, but we are with someone who loves us and won't give up. It's a great picture of the cross.

God does intervene and change situations, miraculously and/or by working through people. But ultimately, his promise is to be with us in the highs and lows. To always be there every day and always be loving.

T Wow, if that picture is true then it's incredible. Gives me a bit of hope.

B It is true. Jesus swapped places and took on our shame and separation and self-loathing. We now stand in his place, in the place of the sinless human who was fully connected to God and neighbour. His resurrection proves he overcomes sin and his way is authentic and leads to life and connection.[14]

T Sorry, I feel bad asking this, but I really need to.

You keep saying that Jesus swapped places with us, that as a human he came down to Earth and experienced our disconnection, but did Jesus really experience rejection, pain, and separation? I mean, can you really say that he stood in humanity's place?

B Well, how long have you got?! Because of the cross, he experienced disconnection in a very real sense. For starters, he was betrayed by a friend he had taught, travelled with, ate with, discipled, and spent most waking minutes with for about three years, Judas Iscariot.[15]

Luke 22:4-6

And Judas went to the chief priests and the officers of the temple guard and discussed with them how he might betray Jesus. They were delighted and agreed to give him money. He consented, and watched for an opportunity to hand Jesus over to them when no crowd was present.

His other friends abandoned him when he was arrested and needed them the most. Peter denied that he even knew him.

Matthew 26:56

. . . Then all the disciples deserted him and fled.

Matthew 26:69-70

Now Peter was sitting out in the courtyard, and a servant-girl came to him. 'You also were with Jesus of Galilee,' she said. But he denied it before them all. 'I don't know what you're talking about,' he said.

He was mocked and humiliated from the time he was arrested until he died, and people were throwing insults at him constantly. His humiliation would have been made worse because he was probably naked as he was nailed on the cross.[16]

In addition, being killed on a cross was in itself seen as a humiliating way to die by the Jews, reserved for worst kinds of people. The Romans thought so, too, and used it to kill the worse type of criminals; the traitors who had rebelled against the state. So Jesus died as a complete outsider. He became the lowest of the low.[17]

Matthew 27:27-30

Then the governor's soldiers took Jesus into the Praetorium and gathered the whole company of soldiers round him. They stripped him and put a scarlet robe on him, and then twisted together a crown of thorns and set it on his head. They put a staff in his right hand. Then they knelt in front of him and mocked him. 'Hail, king of the Jews!' they said. They spit on him, and took the staff and struck him on the head again and again.

Matthew 27:38-41

Two rebels were crucified with him, one on his right and one on his left. Those who passed by hurled insults at him, shaking their heads and saying, 'You who are going to destroy the temple and build it in three days, save yourself! Come down from the cross, if you are the Son of God!' In the same way the chief priests, the teachers of the law and the elders mocked him.

> He was on the receiving end of other people's anger, he was accused falsely, and lied about.

Mark 14:57-59

Then some stood up and gave this false testimony against him: 'We heard him say, "I will destroy this temple made with human hands and in three days will build another, not made with hands."' Yet even then their testimony did not agree.

Luke 23:13-21

Pilate called together the chief priests, the rulers and the people, and said to them, 'You brought me this man as one who was inciting the people to rebellion. I have examined him in your presence and have found *no basis for your charges against him. Neither has Herod, for he sent him back to us; as you can see, he has done nothing to deserve death. Therefore, I will punish him and then release him.' But the whole crowd shouted, 'Away with this man! Release Barabbas to us!' (Barabbas had been thrown into prison for an insurrection in the city, and for murder.) Wanting to release Jesus, Pilate appealed to them again. But they kept shouting, 'Crucify him! Crucify him!'*

God the Father had to reject him because he took on our sin. Jesus knew what it was truly like to be disconnected from God.

Mark 15:34

And at three in the afternoon Jesus cried out in a loud voice, 'Eloi, Eloi, lema sabachthani?' (which means 'My God, my God, why have you forsaken me?')

And I should highlight again that he didn't come to Earth as a semi-God being. He was fully God, but also fully human in order to connect authentically with us on our level. So the physical, emotional and spiritual pain he went through was felt like a human. He did not have a 'divine layer of protection' to make it easier.

Philippians 2:6-7

[Jesus Christ], being in very nature God, did not consider equality with God something to be used to his own advantage; rather, he made

135

himself nothing by taking the very nature of a servant, being made in human likeness.

John 1:14
The Word [Jesus] became flesh and made his dwelling among us.

Jesus experienced, as a human, what it's like to be alone, rejected, abandoned, disconnected. He knows the effects of bad relationships and about the physical pain that comes from hatred, because crucifixion was an awful and painful way to die.[18] He truly stood in the place of disconnection and swapped places with humanity.

T   Wow, that's a lot to take in.

B   Indeed. Sorry to throw so much at you, but I want you to understand that Jesus really did experience disconnection and broken relationships as a human. He took on all of that disconnection, and he stood in the pace of disconnection, even though he did not sin or deserve it.

T   So God the Son, the perfect human, willingly felt the effects of bad, dysfunctional relationships. He experienced the effects of disconnection, so, what, so he could empathise?

B More than that, he did it so that he could put an end to sin and absorb its effects by dying in the place of disconnection. And he also overcame the effects of disconnection.

Remember I said Jesus' death was a sacrifice *for us?* It covers and reverses the damage done by disconnection. It fills in the potholes on a damaged road. The death of the perfect, sinless, fully connected human deals with the negative effects forever.

His resurrection means he is still alive. So Jesus overcame death and he lives, meaning the effects of his sacrifice lead to ongoing and eternal life and connection. He has truly overcome sin forever and can give us a life that is connected with God and others permanently.

---

2 Corinthians 5:17-21

Therefore, if anyone is in Christ, the new creation has come: the old has gone, the new is here! All this is from God, who reconciled us to himself through Christ and gave us the ministry of reconciliation: that God was reconciling the world to himself in Christ, not counting people's sins against them. And he has committed to us the message of reconciliation. We are therefore Christ's ambassadors, as though God were making his appeal through us. We implore you on Christ's behalf: be reconciled to God. God made him who had no sin to be sin for us, so that in him we might become the righteousness of God.

Romans 6:8-11

Now if we died with Christ, we believe that we will also live with him. For we know that since Christ was raised from the dead, he cannot die again; death no longer has mastery over him. The death he died, he died to sin once for all; but the life he lives, he lives to God. In the same way, count yourselves dead to sin but alive to God in Christ Jesus.

T So all the disconnection we cause has really been dealt with, past, present and future? Even when we make mistakes and relate unlovingly as Christians? He can always forgive and restore the relationship?

B Bingo. Jesus has dealt with everything for good and the effects can be experienced right now. The Bible says his death was enough. We need to believe in what Jesus has done and accept his message and what he did because of our own, and everyone's, relational dysfunction.

T So when we sin now, it doesn't matter?

B We will always be forgiven and loved by God, but this doesn't mean believers can keep on sinning and act like it doesn't matter.

Believers are told to live a life that is dedicated towards serving God and honouring him. There is always grace for the believer when we make a mistake, but we must aim to avoid sinning (again) and strive towards God and his purposes.

T Sorry, I know that. What I was trying to say is that even when we relate unlovingly and cause disconnection, it doesn't mean God is going to kick us out of the family.

B Exactly. The cross, the ransom, changes our status and we're now loved children of God. His resurrection proves that he can indeed move us from disconnection to connection because his way leads to life and connection. It's permanently opened the loving relationship with God for us.

You can know you are loved and will always be welcome.

Hebrews 4:14-16

Therefore, since we have a great high priest who has ascended into heaven, Jesus the Son of God, let us hold firmly to the faith we profess. For we do not have a high priest who is unable to feel sympathy for our weaknesses, but we have one who has been tempted in every way, just as we are – yet he did not sin. Let us then approach God's throne of grace with confidence, so that we may receive mercy and find grace to help us in our time of need.

T So the road is permanently fixed. Even if there is something that could cause a pothole or damage, it won't, because Jesus' sacrifice allows for permanent connection, love and good relationships to be a constant. If we believe in him, we can always be connected, right?

B It's like running home to a relative or friend that loves us, wants us to be part of their lives and is always there. We may hurt them. We may hurt others. We may feel unworthy. But all of that doesn't define the relationship anymore. We belong, we're wanted and they are always there now.

T This is incredible! I can't text quick enough! I was planning on just forgetting about God and everything when I woke up this morning. But I just want to ask more!

B Glad to hear it.

T This really is great.

B The cross is understood in many ways by the biblical authors. But in the context of sin as disconnection, like I said before, the effects are:

1: It allows us to have the status and fully loving relationship Jesus had with God, we are fully connected with him. He sees our true selves and will never leave us.

2: Past and future disconnection, relational dysfunction and its effects which separate us have been dealt with and overcome permanently. These things don't define us or create separation now, they are reversed. Connection is here to stay.

T

Sorry to bring this up again, I just want to be clear in my head. Jesus was fully human, but also fully God too, so this means he can bring us into God's family because he is God, right?

B

Yes. Only God can connect us with God. Only a famous person, surrounded by security, can invite us in to their home and show us their true selves. We can't force them. Only God can initiate a connection. He met with us, the motivation and result of the cross is love. We now belong.

T

I always struggled with why Jesus experienced a brutal crucifixion, with lots of blood and gore, and why he needed to die. But this is helping. The idea that it fits in with the wider biblical themes, like sacrifice and ransom, means it wasn't random. The cross matters to me today because it brings that connection. Amazing!

B Exactly. Jesus stood in our place with all of us who feel shame, unworthiness, rejection, and loneliness, and died so that we could stand in his place and lead the life he did. This will change the way we see our enemies, family, friends, what we do with our money, our spare time. A connected life to God changes everything.

We've all sinned and been unloving, but we've also been sinned against and experienced dysfunctional relationships. Jesus' cross and resurrection can overcome all of this, bring forgiveness and transformation and wipe the slate clean, but we need to accept him and put our faith in him.

T This is crazy. It just feels good knowing that God doesn't hate me for asking these questions.

B I know on the surface the cross is quite barbaric and bloody and not nice. But it was for love. Any loving parent would do anything to protect and save the children they love.

T I'm excited, but I'm trying to think about how this will help me at work or when I'm struggling. How should it affect my day-to-day life?

B Remember I said that the cross and resurrection also achieves a third result: We know we're loved, we belong, and are wanted because we are brought into God's loving family, with loving brothers and sisters and a loving father.

Family and community is redefined in light of the cross by Jesus himself. Family is defined by belief in his death and resurrection and nothing else.

John 19:25-27

Near the cross of Jesus stood his mother, his mother's sister, Mary the wife of Clopas, and Mary Magdalene. When Jesus saw his mother there, and the disciple whom he loved standing near by, he said to her, 'Woman, here is your son,' and to the disciple, 'Here is your mother.' From that time on, this disciple took her into his home.

T But why does being brought into a family matter so much? Can't I just connect with God and get on with it?

B Well, no, not really. Jesus gives us his status and we become God's child, but that is also given to our fellow believers. They become our Christian brothers and sisters. This is confirmed by the power of the Holy Spirit.

John 1:12-13

Yet to all who did receive him, to those who believed in his name, he gave the right to become children of God – children born not of natural descent, nor of human decision or a husband's will, but born of God.

John 20:17

Jesus said, 'Do not hold on to me, for I have not yet ascended to the Father. Go instead to my brothers and tell them, "I am ascending to my Father and your Father, to my God and your God."'

Galatians 3:26-28

So in Christ Jesus you are all children of God through faith, for all of you who were baptised into Christ have clothed yourselves with Christ. There is neither Jew nor Gentile, neither slave nor free, nor is there male and female, for you are all one in Christ Jesus.

Galatians 4:6-7

Because you are his sons, God sent the Spirit of his Son into our hearts, the Spirit who calls out, 'Abba, Father.' So you are no longer a slave, but God's child; and since you are his child, God has made you also an heir.

> When we're saved, we aren't given an 'individual' salvation, we're saved into a community, a family. We instinctively know that families should be the place (sadly, many aren't) where we feel safe and receive love. Our family (should) know the real us. See our flaws and still love us. We trust them to always be there.

 T Is that why many churches call themselves family?

B Yes. It's because they realise church should be the place where we can have good, loving, honest relationships and get support. To be human is to be messy, but God and our spiritual family are there to love and help. No Christian is an orphan or only child, you're in the family.

T But church is so often the place where people get hurt. Where we feel like people let us down. I see so many Christians who are hypocrites, who hurt a lot of people, how is that OK? How was it OK when I got hurt by those people?

B Well, it's not. It's not OK. And I really am sorry. God wants Christians to be people who are building good relationships with others. We stand in Jesus' place. Therefore we need to love like he loved. Unfortunately, hurt people hurt people.

The good news is that Jesus has taken on the hurt, and damage, and overcome it. He offers love, forgiveness and reconciliation. We don't define ourselves by the shame, rejection or hurt anymore. His loving, stable relationship can help us to love ourselves and pass on his transforming love to others.

Romans 12:17-21

Do not repay anyone evil for evil. Be careful to do what is right in the eyes of everyone. If it is possible, as far as it depends on you, live at peace with everyone. Do not take revenge, my dear friends, but leave room for God's wrath, for it is written: 'It is mine to avenge; I will repay,' says the Lord. On the contrary:

> *'If your enemy is hungry, feed him; if he is thirsty, give him something to drink.*

In doing this, you will heap burning coals on his head.' Do not be overcome by evil, but overcome evil with good.

T It's not easy, though, is it?

B No, it's not. It's not always easy to accept God's love and realise we're loved and not alone. It isn't easy to stop relating unlovingly to others. It isn't easy to try to restore relationships with those who really hurt us. It's not easy to forgive. It's not easy.

T Thanks for admitting that, Barney.

B We're told to love our enemies. We're told to love the people around us and not to let negative emotions lead us. We're told to treat each other like family. We're saved into a community who are meant to be there for us and love us and vice versa. That's the goal, even though we fall short sometimes.

1 Corinthians 12:25-26

So that there should be no division in the body, but that its parts should have equal concern for each other. If one part suffers, every part suffers with it; if one part is honoured, every part rejoices with it.

Matthew 12:48-50

He replied to him, 'Who is my mother, and who are my brothers?' Pointing to his disciples, he said, 'Here are my mother and my brothers. For whoever does the will of my Father in heaven is my brother and sister and mother.'

1 Peter 3:8-9

Finally, all of you, be like-minded, be sympathetic, love one another, be compassionate and humble. Do not repay evil with evil or insult with insult. On the contrary, repay evil with blessing, because to this you were called so that you may inherit a blessing.

1 Thessalonians 4:9-10

Now about your love for one another we do not need to write to you, for you yourselves have been taught by God to love each other. And in fact, you do love all of God's family throughout Macedonia. Yet we urge you, brothers and sisters, to do so more and more ...

We need to strive towards loving connection because that is what Jesus our Saviour did. The life he led meant he loved everyone fully. His relationships were fully connected.

But we don't do this on our own or in our own strength. We let our permanent connection and loving relationship with God overflow to those around us. His love and closeness transforms our other relationships and brings connection.

T So we treat each other like a family because we're in God's family?

B Bingo. And this love isn't just for Christians, people 'in the club'. We're meant to love everyone, even those who mock us and don't believe what we do. Build relationships with all people. Our family is there for us, loves us and we love them back, and also love people who aren't in the family and aren't believers.

T You're about to say that this is how it should affect me at work, right? I know I'm loved by God and I have brothers and sisters, and we all strive towards fully loving, connected relationships. In turn, we pass this on to others. Like an electric cable that passes on power down the wires. God is the source; we pass on his love.

B I honestly couldn't say it better than that. You're right. It starts with God's love for us.

T So even though it's hard, and they may not be loving to me, I can rely on God to be with me in the hard times. And he will love me and define me as his daughter despite the context or how bad I feel. So instead of running away from him when it gets tough, I need to run towards him.

B That doesn't mean it doesn't matter if we hurt others or they hurt us, but it means that God won't leave us. Through the struggle, he is there. We are his child now and forever, we're always in the loving family. We get our identity from how God sees us.

I will say it again. You're loved by God. That's what this is all about. In our disappointments and failure, God is there. In our hurt and isolation, God is there. You are loved, no matter what, and aren't alone. You're free to fail, to not look perfect, to break the diet, to not get the grades, because the cross brings loving relationships.

T This is really great. God really is good. This is exciting. It's exciting to think that we're called to love other people with the family values. Even if we get hurt, God wants us to try to build good relationships and restore relationships. Life is so messy sometimes, though, but God is right in the mess.

B God doesn't promise us ease and comfort, but he does promise to be there. We aren't alone, we are wanted, and he is with us. The cross and resurrection restores relationships.

T Even though some situations are hard, I now know I'm not alone! A fully connected, loving relationship with God defines me and affects me in every way. And my brothers and sisters are there too. Even though families sometimes do fight.

B Yes. The cross really is like coming home to a family member or dear friend who hugs you and makes you feel valued. That's the feeling God wants you to have in your relationship with him.

T This is a bit overwhelming, in a good way, though. I think I'm beginning to see why Jesus died, it was so he could establish real and ongoing connection. A connection that is reliable and can change my situation today. The relationship the cross offers changes everything.

I'm feeling like I did when I became a Christian again, like I absolutely need God in my life, I'm seeing Jesus in a whole new way.

B We do need Jesus, we need his cross. It brings forgiveness of sins because it overcomes the relational dysfunction we cause and suffer. It bring connection because the barriers and problems between us and God, and the damage we cause to others and vice versa, has been dealt with and covered over in his death and sacrifice.

We can't fix it on our own. We can't deal with the disconnection on our own. This isn't 'relationship counselling'. Jesus sorted it, not us. Without him we stay disconnected forever. He brings the connection we crave, he answers our need, and we can take hold of that reality when we believe in what he has done for us.

Mark 2:17

On hearing this, Jesus said to them, 'It is not the healthy who need a doctor, but those who are ill. I have not come to call the righteous, but sinners.'

The cross and resurrection restores relationships. Jesus dies to pay the cost of forgiveness and establishes a fully connected relationship, and it means you will always be loved, no matter what. You get the status Jesus had, so you're now a child of God and you're brought into God's loving family.

T   I really can believe God is close now. I can begin to see that he really loves me. Thank you, Barney. I feel like I want to pray about everything and ask God to help.

B   Good. What will you pray for?

T Thank God that he cares about my situation. That he is there for me, even when it gets hard and I feel like ignoring him. And even when I get hurt at work, and probably hurt others, he loves me and wants to help me through it. I'm defined by being in his family and not the disconnection.

I even want him to help me connect with my colleagues at work.

B I also pray that you experience his love more, too.

T What do you mean, experience it? I know he loves me, isn't that more important?

B Well, would you want a boyfriend or good friend to just write down facts about themselves? Or do you want to hang out with them, do things together and get to know each other?

A relationship isn't just head knowledge, it's an experience and feeling. So ask God to reveal himself to you, to show you he loves you. Go to church and experience a loving, connected family, for example. Or ask him to show you he is close and loving.

T This really has helped so much. I can't believe how excited I feel about all this. God really does love me. The cross is all about God's love from start to end. In fact, I'm going to come out with you guys. I want to be part of the family! I want to experience it and belong. Is that OK?

B Yes, I'm actually running late and about to leave. We're meeting at the normal place. They're all there already.

T Sorry! I'm the one who made you late. Sorry. I'm going to quickly walk the dog, I will see you there. I was going to ask more about what being part of the family looks like.

B Let's talk about it face-to-face. It's a really important question. Being part of the family is about more than just 'being nice'. It has so many more consequences. The cross is the beginning of our new life and purpose, we now get to change this world and bring heaven down to earth!

T Wow, this sounds amazing. Let's chat about it some more in a bit.

Current status
Thank you God for always being there, even when I have questions. I can't stop singing this worship song now!

'I have been redeemed
I've been set free
Pulled from the sea
And You came
And brought me in
Defeated my sin
And called me Your friend

Now I'm alive in You God
I'm in the family now
I'm satisfied in You God
Your love is everything

No longer slave to sin and death
You stepped right down into my mess
He ransomed me and paid my debts
And clothed me in His righteousness

My sin does not belong to me
The King of Love has set me free
He's taken off my filthy rags
And brought me in the family

Now I'm alive in You God
I'm in the family now
I'm satisfied in You God
Your love is everything'

'In the Family' by Rivers and Robots. Composer: Jonathan Ogden. Publisher: Arkyard

Author's Notes

I think some people will read this book and say, 'I already know I'm a son or daughter of God.' Or, 'I know God is with me and loves me.' So this whole Connection Model thing may feel a bit over the top, but the point I'm trying to make is that the answer to disconnection, unworthiness, loneliness, feeling unwanted and separation, is found in the cross and resurrection *itself*.

The answer to this struggle and need is not an afterthought to the 'forgiveness of sins', it's part of the forgiveness. It's not just an added extra or a peripheral point, it's a vital part of Jesus' death and resurrection. The Connection Model can help us remember this amazing truth.

Key Takeaways

- The cross and resurrection allows us to have the status and fully loving relationship Jesus had with God, we are fully connected with him. He sees our true selves and will never leave us.

- Past and future disconnection, relational dysfunction and its effects which separate us have been dealt with and overcome permanently. These things don't define us or create separation now, they are reversed. Connection is here to stay.

- We know we're loved, we belong and are wanted because we are brought into God's loving family, with loving brothers and sisters and a loving father.

- The resurrection proves Jesus' authenticity. It proves what Jesus said and does leads to life because he is still alive, so the effects from his resurrection are permanent and ongoing.

Real Life Stories

It's probably time I share my own testimony with you.

I became a Christian when I was in high school. I was desperate to fit in. I could list all the aspects I didn't like about myself, my looks, my body, my personality. I never felt good enough. So I just tried to fit in with different people, wear different 'masks' to hang out with different social groups. I never let anyone see the real me because I didn't think they would stick around if they did.

I felt lonely and had nowhere to really belong.

Then I was dragged to church by a mate one day, and I met with God in a powerful way and I really enjoyed the church. So I started going regularly. But I didn't really become a Christian until a few months later. Looking back, though, it was hearing that there was a God who loved me unconditionally, who called me his child, who saw all my flaws and mistakes and bits I didn't like about me, and said I was still in the family.

He knew the real me, but said I was still loved and accepted. He said he would never leave, and he never has.

It's this unwavering, unrelenting, unlimited love that has shaped my life. It far outweighs anything else I've ever pursued or come across. This relational understanding of God, and knowing I'm in the family, no matter what, because of what Jesus did on the cross, changed everything for me. It's a big reason why I'm writing this book.

Real Life Application

I think we often focus so much on legal forgiveness, we forget that the forgiveness of sins Jesus brings encompasses so much.

God's forgiveness does bring legal forgiveness and that's important. But as said before, God's forgiveness 'wipes the slate clean' and does many things at once.

This should lead us to realise how much we need Jesus.

He overcomes so much for us. This truth only becomes a reality in our daily lives when we put our faith in Jesus and accept his cross and resurrection. We need to realise we've suffered and caused disconnection, and need him to reverse the damage this relational dysfunction does and has done. Only Jesus can do this.

When we're thinking we're the worst Christian because we're still getting things wrong and we thought it would be different this time; or we think God's patience must have run out by now; or when we sit in the pew, knowing we're 'saved' but wondering how we, on our own, solve the problem of feeling unlovable, separated, alone, unworthy, disconnected, we need to remind ourselves God is always our loving father and friend. We're always welcomed by him. This cannot change because the cross and resurrection restores relationships.

Some helpful questions to ask at this point:

- Have I put my faith in what Jesus did, and said sorry for the disconnection I caused, and decided to connect and build a relationship with God?

- How can I make sure I never take the cross and resurrection for granted, and am constantly overwhelmed by what God did?

- In times when I feel distant, how can I remind myself that as a Christian, I'm part of the family, *always,* no matter what?

Key Bible Verses

Romans 5:8; John 3:16-17; Hebrews 4:15; Leviticus 17:11; Hebrews 9:22-28; Matthew 20:28; 2 Corinthians 5:17-21; Galatians 4:6-7.

Further Reading

Author Unknown, 'The Long Silence', Lambert Dolphin's Library website, 21 November 1995, http://www.ldolphin.org/silence.html (accessed 27.2.18).

Flood, D., 'A Relational Understanding of Atonement', in Montgomery, B., Oord, T. J., and Winslow, K.S. (eds.), Relational Theology: A Contemporary Introduction, Eugene, OR: Wipf & Stock, 2012, 40-42.

Macleod, D., Christ Crucified: Understanding the Atonement, Nottingham: IVP, 2014.

Wilson, B.R., 'The Crucifixion Scene as the Climax of Lukan Inclusively', Expository Times 127 (June 2016), 430-438.

Chapter 3

'Does my life matter?'
Christ imparts purpose

Amy

Age 26

Work/Education
Read Business. Work as a Commodity Broker (think investment banking, salesperson, and logistics mixed with stress!)

About me
I'm playful, giggly, boisterous, addicted to smiling, and the combo of chocolate and films always wins. I spend my weeks working very hard (and too many weekends as well!) but when I can, I attend fabulous parties and enjoy getting into trouble.
    Prosecco made me do it!

What's the one question you would ask God?
I know you're not there, but why would you create wasps?!

Current status
I've been reminded of how lovely all my friends are. You're all amazing!

PART 1

> **A** Hi Barney, how are you? I'm not in work because I have some annual leave to use up. Just relaxing today. Thought I would see how you're doing.

> **B** Hi, Amy. I'm good, thanks. I haven't seen you in a while. I think the last time was at the summer festival. I hope you're enjoying yourself. I've just got on the train, taking a long weekend and going to visit family. Back for the Sunday service, though! Have you been away anywhere?

> **A** I haven't gone away, just had a stress-free week at home. Been catching up with friends I haven't seen in ages and it's been great. I met up with your lot from your church last night too. I haven't seen many of them since that festival, and I haven't laughed so much in a long time.

> **B** Was this at the last-minute thing Tina organised? Unfortunately I couldn't go. Who went in the end?

> **A** Yeah it was at Tina's. Someone told her I was off and she said I should come too, which was nice of her. I don't really know her that well but she was very welcoming.

> Tina seemed different from what I remembered. Much more confident and happy. She never

struck me as someone to host or organise a big social thing like that. But she seemed like she really enjoyed it. Well, until Toby spilt his drink all over her new rug!

B Oh no! Was she OK? Poor Tina. Toby is so energetic. No doubt he was jumping around unable to sit still, as usual. We met up the other day, he's back from uni because it's reading week.

A I was surprised to see him. She was fine actually, very calm about her rug. She mainly didn't want Toby to feel bad. I would be fuming! But everyone was so friendly, and everyone seemed so together. They really seem to belong, I guess. It made me feel like I was missing something.

B What do you mean by that?

A Well it just seemed like they're doing what they're meant to be doing, if that makes sense? Take Toby, we both know he needs an off switch sometimes, but he is just so passionate about God. Whenever he talks about God he gets super-animated.

I just feel like I'm missing something, or missing my purpose. I sat there thinking; I go to work, I come home, but does my life really matter? It kept me up most of the night too, and you know I like my beauty sleep.

B No one has life sorted, I can tell you that for sure. But knowing God wants to connect is an amazing truth that shapes how 'us church lot' live our lives.

A Toby was talking about this. It's why I'm messaging you, actually. You know I don't believe in Jesus or anything, but I just couldn't stop thinking about what Toby said. And how Toby and Tina have changed.

You always said you were happy to chat about God and stuff. I hope you don't mind? I just can't shake this feeling. I'm suddenly thinking about my purpose. I mean, does my life matter? Am I making a difference? I didn't know who else to talk to. I trust you, and no one else would understand.

B Let me give you a call. It may be easier to chat on the phone.

Sorry, Amy. The phone cut out twice and I couldn't hear you at all. I think the signal is temperamental because of the train. We may have to just message each other for now. Sorry. What was Toby saying exactly?

A Yeah, that call was a bit of a fail! That's fine. I'm just at home anyway. Well, Toby started talking about how sin isn't just about 'the bad stuff we do', but it's also about disconnection, like when we feel unworthy. He said that the cross ultimately allows him to connect with God and others, and restore relationships. Does that sound right?

B Yes, it does. It's nice to know he's taken on board some of the things we've been chatting about, and he's thinking it through for himself.

A Then he started saying something about how the resurrection proves Jesus' way can bring us life right now. And even though Christians will die physically, this 'life' brings a relationship with God and a connection free from sin and disconnection.

Usually I wouldn't listen to all this, but Toby just looks like he's doing what he's meant to be doing. How come his belief in Jesus gives him this sense of purpose?

I mean, I always thought Christians just did nice things while they waited to die and go to heaven, or the afterlife, or whatever. I thought they just waited. But Toby was saying there's more to it. It's about getting a connection now, not just when you die and go to heaven. Then we got interrupted and didn't finish talking about it.

B Going to be with God after we die, going to heaven and the afterlife will happen in the future, but Jesus has *already* been resurrected back to life. So he's *already* overcome the effects of sin and disconnection. Meaning God can build loving relationships with us now, and start building his kingdom on Earth right now.

A What do you mean, 'building his kingdom on Earth'? Sounds like some strategy gaming app.

B Sorry, I know that's a strange phrase. In the Bible, I see it teaching me that God will ultimately come down to this earth and live among his people.[1] His people will see God's face and have a relationship free from shame, isolation and dysfunction, with him and everyone else. We won't just get transported to a cloud with a harp.

Revelation 21:2-4

I saw the Holy City, the new Jerusalem, coming down out of heaven from God, prepared as a bride beautifully dressed for her husband. And I heard a loud voice from the throne saying, 'Look! God's dwelling-place is now among the people, and he will dwell with them. They will be his people, and God himself will be with them and be their God. "He will wipe every tear from their eyes. There will be no more death" or mourning or crying or pain, for the old order of things has passed away.'

God's 'kingdom', this place where God lives, rules, and relates to us without barriers, will be established fully at the end of time by God and God alone.

However, Jesus' resurrection allows us to be used by God to start partially establishing it now. We get to start building his kingdom with him now, in this life. Laying the foundations for when he fully establishes it.

A What are you trying to build, exactly? What is 'laying the foundations'?

B Well, think of it like this: God will one day dwell with us, love us and connect fully with no barriers and no sin getting in the way. We will also relate to each in fully loving relationship too. As Christians, we want that future reality to impact this life as much as possible. It's not just for after we die.

Christians don't just do 'nice things' to stay on God's good side so we get a ticket into heaven. God chooses to use us and work through us, so we can be part of building his kingdom, defined by fully connected, loving relationships. A place free from disconnection.[2]

A So all those loving acts you church lot (should) do, bring and reflect some of that future kingdom in the here and now?

B Exactly. Picture a room: it's pitch black and it's the middle of the night. There's absolutely no light in the room. As the sun rises, some light comes in through the cracks in the blinds. As the sun rises more, more light comes in. When the sun is fully up and someone fully opens the blinds, the whole room is lit up.

Similarly, whenever people connect with God or others, when they relate lovingly, some of God's future kingdom breaks in, some light comes in through the blinds. When Jesus returns he will open the blinds fully and establish his kingdom of full connection on earth. That's a picture of what I call heaven coming down to Earth.

A So this is what drives you? This is why you try to do nice things even when there is so much rubbish in the world?

B Just like in that room, there is still darkness in this world and in our lives. Rubbish things happen. But we're invited by God to work with him, and we can bring some of the light in, and it makes a difference.

It's not just about 'being nice', it's about being part of something that will have eternal consequences. Actively choosing to live by God's will, and his standards, rather than our own.

Revelation 22:3-5

No longer will there be any curse. The throne of God and of the Lamb will be in the city, and his servants will serve him. They will see his face, and his name will be on their foreheads. There will be no more night. They will not need the light of a lamp or the light of the sun, for the Lord God will give them light. And they will reign for ever and ever.

A I do envy you guys sometimes. I type away at my computer at work and meet up with clients, do all of this overtime, see the money in my bank account rise, but I miss my friends. I thought this job was it, the big prize. But I just feel so lonely sometimes.

B There's nothing wrong with getting a good job and money in the bank. However, sometimes we forget what should really matter, and what should come first.

A But how do I know what should matter? You make it sound so simple, but actually it's hard to know what I should be doing.

B Put it like this, what sort of things do you see written on tombstones?

A That's an odd question, even for you! But I guess you see 'Beloved father', or 'Much loved wife and mother', or 'Dear friend'.

B Exactly. You never see 'Here lies the woman who made a million pounds'. Or 'Here lies the man who owned a big house'. In the end, relationships seem to be what matters. It's what people are remembered for.

A I remember someone saying that in our culture we're taught to rigorously look after our cars: get a yearly MOT, check our oil regularly, check the tyres and so on. Yet friendships, marriages and relationships are left to drift and sort themselves out.[3] We're rarely taught how to maintain relationships. That always stuck with me.

B I always say that we want relationships to last but we leave it to chance. We put them in last place behind other things and get caught up in the busyness of life.

I truly believe the life, death and resurrection of Jesus can answer that need we deeply crave: gaining a deep, unconditional, loving relationship. The cross brings us into a family, and into a connection with God, which also transforms and restores all of our relationships. As we relate differently, we bring connection.

A So do you think the cross was all about building relationships, then?

B Do you remember that talk we had on the coach, and you joked that the cross was like a multicoloured toolbox? I've used that phrase a lot since then.

A How could I forget?! You said the cross was both beautiful and useful in many different ways, and then I thought about where I could get a multicoloured toolbox from.

B Well, I think the life of Jesus, the cross and resurrection achieved many things and we're just talking about and emphasising one element. One colour in the beautiful rainbow. One tool in the toolbox.[4] But I do think overcoming disconnection and establishing connection and loving relationships is key to answering your questions.

A If I'm being honest, and I don't mean to offend, it sounds like Jesus is just telling you to go off and build good relationships. It just sounds like he's giving good advice. What if this kingdom stuff is wrong and it's just some helpful wisdom? Joke's on you, isn't it?

B This is more than some good advice because loving relationships, love itself, is at the core of who God is.

Christians believe in a triune God, this means he is one God but three persons. God the Father, God the Son and God the Holy Spirit, all distinct but one. This means that God within himself lives in constant loving relationship. The Father loves the Son, the Son loves the Spirit, etc. God's very core is a loving connection.

A But why would that matter?

B God seems to have designed humanity and made us to reflect this loving relationship. To reflect who he is. We are designed, among other things, to live in loving relationships, too.

Genesis 2:18

The LORD God said, 'It is not good for the man to be alone . . . '

Genesis 1:26-28

Then God said, 'Let us make mankind in our image, in our likeness, so that they may rule over the fish in the sea and the birds in the sky, over the livestock and all the wild animals, and over all the creatures that move along the ground.' So God created mankind in his own image, in the image of God he created them; male and female he created them. God blessed them and said to them . . . '

When God made humans, the togetherness and plurality was emphasised. The Bible seems to teach that God lives in loving relationships. He exists in the context of love and relationships; and he wants us to experience that with him and others.

God's kingdom isn't built on some random helpful advice, but on the nature of God himself.[5]

A   I thought that Christians just did good things to stay on God's good side. I always like the way you talk about God, Barney.

B   Thank you. I just hope it's helping. Does all this 'God choosing to build his kingdom with us and through us' stuff make sense?

A   Yeah. Basically, you think God himself lives in loving relationships and he designed humans to live in loving relationships too. When you make connections, God uses this to build his kingdom and bring some of heaven to Earth. Which God will fully bring down in the future. Have I got it? Is that everything?

B Well, there is more detail we could go into and other important elements to it, but yeah, what you said is essential to understanding what the kingdom of God is. Especially when we emphasise the problem of disconnection.

We now get to relate and connect to God. This isn't some self-help process, God connects with us and it has a profound effect. Our purpose and new life is rooted in a real connection with the living God. He could do it without us, but he invites us to be part of building his kingdom, bringing in light, and this has eternal consequences.

As we connect with the designer, we realise what we're designed for.

A But why the cross, then? Why not just connect to God?

B The cross is vital because even though we've suffered the effects of relational dysfunction and disconnection, we've nevertheless been unloving in our relationships at times, too. This sin, this disconnection, causes pain and damage. It creates shame, separations and creates barriers between people, and between us and God.

So God paid the price and sorted it. He defeated death, overcame the disconnection and allowed humanity to connect with him again. If we choose to believe in what he's done, we can connect with him and allow it to transform how we connect with others.

A And you really think that someone needs to put their faith in Jesus dying on the cross? That only Jesus can bring this life and purpose you're talking about?

B Yes, I do. Jesus isn't an optional extra or some good advice. I always say: Christ imparts purpose. Through his birth, life, death and resurrection we're saved, forgiven and offered new life, and shown how to live this new life. I believe that this new life means:

1: Christians get a new identity and a new kingdom-building purpose.

2: We follow the example of Jesus with the help of the Holy Spirit.

3: We grow the family by telling people about God and his desire to connect and by demonstrating the family values by loving all people.

A Sorry, Barney, you lost me. Can you explain these points please?

B It starts with a new identity. The cross and resurrection allows us to connect with God and shows us that we're wanted. The disconnection and self-loathing we feel doesn't have the final say because God sees us and loves us and deals with sin.

We're all aware of our flaws and what we do wrong. We can all wear masks and cover up who we are because we're scared people won't love the real us. But the connection with God changes our identity and how we see ourselves.

A But I believe that sometimes we need to 'put on a mask'. At a job interview we need to be more professional than we are at home. Or in some situations we need to do something our personality wouldn't naturally lead us to. Like if someone shy goes to a party, they may make the effort to be more outgoing.

Or let's say a doctor went to work feeling like they just wanted to sit around in their pyjamas all day and eat chocolate. You would hope that they would wear appropriate clothes and act professionally, even if they felt like doing something else. I don't want a doctor with chocolate stains all over their face!

B I definitely agree with your last point! I do get what you're saying, but the problem is, if the gap between our real self and the mask(s) gets too big, or we wear it for too long, it's harder for us to love ourselves. Or believe someone else might.

Sadly, we're reminded of our flaws every day. Hundreds of years ago most people lived in small villages or towns and were surrounded by a few dozen people. Now modern technology means we see images and hear stories about thousands of people every day. Lots of them remind us we aren't as good, and it brings disconnection.

A Yeah, I can identify with that.

B But Christians get a new identity. This is important because it's crucial to understand God loves us and makes us a new creation. He brings us into his loving family, so we must see ourselves differently and understand that we can take off the mask because God won't leave us.

Romans 8:38-39

For I am convinced that neither death nor life, neither angels nor demons, neither the present nor the future, nor any powers, neither height nor depth, nor anything else in all creation, will be able to separate us from the love of God that is in Christ Jesus our Lord.

---

2 Corinthians 5:17

Therefore, if anyone is in Christ, the new creation has come: the old has gone, the new is here!

> The Bible says that believers are now royalty and God's special possession rather than strangers. We're children of the light. We're chosen by him, we're not a mistake, and so much more. We're made new and get a new identity.

1 Peter 2:9-10

But you are a chosen people, a royal priesthood, a holy nation, God's special possession, that you may declare the praises of him who called you out of darkness into his wonderful light. Once you were not a people, but now you are the people of God; once you had not received mercy, but now you have received mercy.

1 Thessalonians 5:5

You are all children of the light and children of the day. We do not belong to the night or to the darkness.

Ephesians 1:4

For he chose us in him before the creation of the world to be holy and blameless in his sight ...

> God sees the real us and knows we're far from perfect and have major struggles, but we're still part of his family, no matter what. We can still belong and connect.

Our life is not defined by the old or the negative labels. We don't need to be a 'failure', 'ugly', 'an outsider', 'strange', 'an addict', 'not good enough', 'unlovable', 'untalented', 'stupid' or anything else anymore. God loves us and wants his sons and daughters to be involved in building his kingdom of connection, and to love others.

A I thought being a Christian was about going to church, celebrating Christmas, wearing a crucifix necklace, and that stuff.

B That's what people often think. Yet Jesus says that the world will know people are Christians if they love each other. Interesting, right? Our loving actions are the main criteria.

John 13:34-35

A new command I [Jesus] give you: love one another. As I have loved you, so you must love one another. By this everyone will know that you are my disciples, if you love one another.

Matthew 25:34-40

Then [Jesus] the King will say to those on his right, 'Come, you who are blessed by my Father; take your inheritance, the kingdom prepared for you since the creation of the world. For I was hungry and you gave me something to eat, I was thirsty and you gave me something to drink, I was a stranger and you invited me in, I needed clothes and you clothed me, I was ill and you looked after me, I was in prison and you came to visit me.' Then the righteous will answer him, 'Lord, when did we see

you hungry and feed you, or thirsty and give you something to drink?'...
The King will reply, 'Truly I tell you, whatever you did for one of the
least of these brothers and sisters of mine, you did for me.'

A I didn't know that.

B God offers us a connection. An unconditional, loving relationship we can rely on. This transforms our identity, and this also brings a new purpose because we're called to pass this love on.[6]

This isn't about being a good person by the world's standards, but loving the world with God's love, connecting with him first, looking to Jesus and relying on his love and grace as we love others. That's the purpose we find.

Loving God and our neighbour helps to build God's kingdom, one which has no disconnection in it, and one that God will fully establish forever. So what we do has eternal consequences and it matters, it's not just random. You can join in, you know, God wants you to be involved, too.

A I just couldn't love people or be that nice all the time. I just couldn't do it. I enjoy spoiling myself too much!

B Well, this loving connection, this wonderful gospel message, is what drives me, not some hollow rules I need to try to keep to stay on God's good side.

A But hang on, all the Christians I know say they need to read their Bible. They need to go to church, they need to be loving even if they find someone hard work. So there are rules? It isn't all about 'love', is it?

B Well, this is often misunderstood. If people read their Bible, pray, or are 'nice' to someone to 'tick off' a rule they need to follow, then that's just about doing empty rituals.

I think people do empty rituals when they want to get a reward or avoid punishment. So if people do things to 'get into heaven' or to avoid 'God not liking them anymore', that's empty rituals.

But I'm talking about something different. Loving people and serving God, connecting and building loving relationships even when it's hard, is what the Bible often calls obedience. This is actually to do with my second point about how Christ imparts purpose. 'We follow the example of Jesus with the help of the Holy Spirit.'

A Obedience to me just means harsh, unloving rules.

B I disagree, obedience in the Bible is about a loving response.

Like I said, God gives us a new identity and brings us into a family. That love, that safety, that freedom, changes us. So we *respond* by loving God and loving others. Even when it doesn't feel easy. Even when it's hard. It's about more than feelings, but choosing to connect.

For example, a husband and wife know they're loved by each other, even during the hard times when they feel negative towards each other because of stress, or a bad situation, or whatever. In those hard times they can choose to respond with acts of love, despite the current negative feelings.

A I think I see what you mean. You're saying following empty rituals is about trying to get something, but obedience in the Bible is about responding to God's love in the right way, in the ups and downs of life. Am I right?

B Yes, well put. To an outsider it looks the same. But obedience is about responding to the love God has shown us, with the help of the Holy Spirit. Choosing connection over disconnection. Even if we don't feel like it all the time.

I believe Jesus lived an authentic human life in obedience to God. In other words, he responded constantly to the loving connection he had to God the Father.

John 15:9-10

As the Father has loved me, so have I loved you. Now remain in my love. If you keep my commands, you will remain in my love, just as I have kept my Father's commands and remain in his love.

John 5:19-24

Jesus gave them this answer: 'Very truly I tell you, the Son can do nothing by himself; he can do only what he sees his Father doing, because whatever the Father does the Son also does. For the Father loves the Son and shows him all he does ... Very truly I tell you, whoever hears my word and believes him who sent me has eternal life and will not be judged but has crossed over from death to life.'

2 John 5-6

... I am not writing you a new command but one we have had from the beginning. I ask that we love one another. And this is love: that we walk in obedience to his commands. As you have heard from the beginning, his command is that you walk in love.

This means the way Jesus connected to God and others is the example for how we should live our new life. Male or female, rich or poor, it doesn't matter. He responded correctly to God's love. He was obedient.

A So the standards you try to live by are the ones you see exampled in Jesus' life.

B Exactly, we know this will ultimately fulfil us and bring connection because Jesus' resurrection proves his way leads to life. He shows us how to build loving, connected relationships.

A But I really couldn't do this because it does sounds like you need to be perfect and loving all the time. And anyway, it sounds to me like love is the key element, and don't all religions basically say this, too? I mean 'why can't we all just get along, man'!

B Well, I believe we can only connect to God by believing in Jesus' message and what he did. He reveals God in his life, and in his death Jesus deals with the disconnection and relational dysfunction. Jesus isn't an optional extra. He brings the connection with God and leaves his Spirit to help us, even though we aren't perfect.

A Leaves his Spirit? Christian jargon alert!

B Guilty. Sorry, let me explain. Have you heard of the phrase, 'My body is a temple'?

A Being the health freak that I am (or was), I definitely have. It means remembering that we need to look after ourselves and try to keep fit, do exercise, stay healthy, that sort of thing.

B Well, that's not what it originally meant. The Bible says God had a temple in Jerusalem, and his Spirit and presence was very tangible in that space. But after Jesus, the Bible writers taught that the believers' bodies are the new temple, our bodies are the new place where God's Spirit is tangible and present.

God is so close and with us always, we're no longer separated by anything because God's Holy Spirit is with us and he helps us to love others. Even when we fail to love others fully, he is there. He is with us even though we aren't perfect.

---

1 Corinthians 6:19-20

Do you not know that your bodies are temples of the Holy Spirit, who is in you, whom you have received from God? You are not your own; you were bought at a price. Therefore honour God with your bodies.

2 Corinthians 6:16

What agreement is there between the temple of God and idols? For we are the temple of the living God. As God has said: 'I will live with them and walk among them, and I will be their God, and they will be my people.'

Galatians 5:22-25

But the fruit of the Spirit is love, joy, peace, forbearance, kindness, goodness, faithfulness, gentleness and self-control. Against such things there is no law. Those who belong to Christ Jesus have crucified the flesh with its passions and desires. Since we live by the Spirit, let us keep in step with the Spirit.

A But most religions do say be a good person and love others and you'll get rewarded. Why is this so different? Why does this give your life such meaning?

B Put it like this: Christianity is different because it's not like a test. It doesn't say work hard, study hard and be a good person, then if you pass and get an A grade, you'll be rewarded. It says you have an A, you've passed, now enjoy the A and act like you have an A.

A And Jesus gives you that A grade?

B Exactly. And it's bad when Christians relate unlovingly and let people down, but no one, Christian or non-Christian, is always loving. We all cause disconnection. But when you believe in Jesus, God has sorted it, so he can still give us an A.

But not only that, God even gives us his Holy Spirit, gives us himself because we are the new temple. Crucially, the Holy Spirit that dwells in the believers' bodies is the same Spirit that guided and connected Jesus to God. The really amazing thing is that Jesus isn't only the example, but the same Spirit that was with him now helps us.

Romans 8:11

And if the Spirit of him who raised Jesus from the dead is living in you, he who raised Christ from the dead will also give life to your mortal bodies because of his Spirit who lives in you.

John 20:21-22

Again Jesus said, 'Peace be with you! As the Father has sent me, I am sending you.' And with that he breathed on them and said, 'Receive the Holy Spirit.'

John 14:14-18; 25-27

... And I will ask the Father, and he will give you another advocate to help you and be with you for ever – the Spirit of truth. The world cannot accept him, because it neither sees him nor knows him. But you know him, for he lives with you and will be in you. I will not leave you as orphans; I will come to you ... All this I [Jesus] have spoken while still with you. But the Advocate, the Holy Spirit, whom the Father will send in my name, will teach you all things and will remind you of everything I have said to you. Peace I leave with you; my peace I give you. I do not give to you as the world gives. Do not let your hearts be troubled and do not be afraid.

His Spirit reminds us that we're connected to him. He'll inspire, encourage and actively help us through his Spirit to pass his loving connection on and overcome the disconnection around us.

A So you think that as a Christian, God gives you an A grade, and you get help living like you have an A grade through his Spirit?

B Exactly. On the cross God dealt with past and future disconnect. His life on earth showed us how to live a fully connected and fulfilling human life with the Holy Spirit. So God builds his kingdom through us when we follow this example. Christ imparts purpose. 'We follow the example of Jesus with the help of the Holy Spirit.'

A Barney, you make this sound so good. I wish I had your faith sometimes, and feel like you do. When you talk, it just all seems to tie in together. It sounds like you have a focus and direction for your life.

B As we connect with the designer, we realise what we're designed for.

God is the most important thing in my life; I try to live his way with his help. He loves you just as much as he loves me, or anyone.

A But what's the catch? This all seems a bit too good to me, if I'm honest with you, Barney.

B I know it seems like that. In one sense there is no catch, God loves you and wants to connect and build his kingdom with you. But I would say that the catch is that God never says life will be easy. God may ask us to do things we don't want to do, like love our enemies, or make hard choices, or forgive people who've really hurt us.

Sometimes we will suffer and go against what other people do or believe. Obedience sometimes means going against what seems logical or doing what makes 'me' comfortable. But Jesus is our Lord and Saviour, he is the King of the kingdom, and his rule and will is what we prioritise above everything else.

Matthew 6:9-10

This, then, is how you should pray: 'Our Father in heaven, hallowed be your name, your kingdom come, your will be done, on earth as it is in heaven.'

I mean, Jesus himself told his followers to pick up their cross and follow him.[7] Before God fully establishes his kingdom, life can still be hard and messy. God can't promise you a painless life, but he can promise you an unbreakable loving connection.

A Sounds like lots of fun!

B Well, you asked for the catch! But the Christian life isn't about being sad or happy all the time. It's about being real and authentic. The point is we have no masks, we have a new identity and we're connected. We're loved. This brings purpose and true life, wherever it leads.

A Is that why you lot do some crazy countercultural things? Like selling your house and going overseas to help the poor? Or choosing to take a harder job that will help more people, even if another job offer has more money? I remember some ridiculous stories from the summer festival.

B Yeah, sometimes. And let's not forget, many Christians in other countries get put in jail, killed and persecuted because of their faith.[8] It's not always easy.

A To be honest, Barney, there was a part of me that hoped you would just say some 'strange' Christian things that would remind me why I don't go to church. And make my concerns go away so I could sleep tonight. Annoyingly, I think you will keep me awake even more.

B I would say sorry, but I'm glad I've got you thinking.

A I hope you aren't expecting me to get on my knees and repent. I'm not sure what 'repent' exactly means, but you Christians always use it.

B 'Repent' literally means 'turning around'. Which sums up what I've said, really. We don't just receive God's love and then continue to head towards relating unloving. We must turn around, change direction and relate differently. This does take time, we'll make mistakes, but Christians need to follow Jesus' example more and more.

We no longer hold grudges, act selfishly, use people, treat God like he's an optional extra. We change. We repent. We experience and let others experience God's radical love, and grow the family.

A Why does this whole growing the family thing matter so much? You mentioned this before, and I did feel like I was part of a family last night. There was something I can't quite explain.

B It's so important. Growing the family is a vital part of our purpose. But they've just announced that my stop is the next one. I need to change trains at this station. I'll call or message you again in a bit.

A OK, no rush. But I want to know about this family thing.

Part 2

B Hi, Amy, you still free to chat?

A I was just wondering if you'd forgotten me. I sorted out the washing, made myself a cup of tea and was answering a few work emails. It's bad, but I feel like I need to stay on top of them. Even on my days off.

B Sorry, train was a bit delayed. Managed to find the platform all right, though. Just found myself a seat, too.

A With your sense of direction, finding the platform may prove there is a God after all!

B Very funny! It's not that bad. Did you manage to sort out your emails?

A Yeah, I did. Well, enough for now, anyway. But I'm trying to process everything you said.

I followed most of it. I must say that I didn't agree with it all. But I want to know what this growing the family thing means.

B Like I said before, essentially, 'We grow the family by telling people about God and his desire to connect and by demonstrating the family values by loving all people.'

We're told not to keep God to ourselves, but to tell others about his family, and demonstrate his love to them by relating to them with the love he gives us.

A You're talking about getting people to church and stuff, aren't you? Getting them to become Christians and accept Jesus. 'Being saved.'

B Yeah. The fancy word is 'evangelism', but yeah. As Christians we want others to hear about and experience the fully loving, connected relationships we have with God. Which they can have, too. We tell them about it, and we connect and love our neighbour as ourselves so they experience it. It's an amazing privilege.

Take last night and what you said about seeing Toby and Tina and hanging out with that group. You were experiencing the family.

A It did feel good. I felt like I belonged. I felt like someone cared. I felt like I could find support. It was just... nice. It was welcoming.

B This is a consequence of the cross for Christians. We find meaning in the call to love and connect with those around us. Whether we buy a gift for a friend, for example, or help deliver aid to a war-torn country, or hang out together. We want to bring light in and build God's kingdom of connection and relate lovingly.

A Come on, Barney! You can't really compare hanging out with friends to people who do something big, like people going from safe countries to help feed the homeless in a poverty-stricken country?!

How can what I experienced last night be the same? That's what I don't get about this whole building God's kingdom thing. How can you compare small, loving acts and relationships to big ones and say they all matter?

B You're right. Obviously there is a difference in one sense. But both of these things are about bringing connection. They are both bringing in light, and God builds his kingdom through us because it gets rid of disconnection. Sometimes we focus on the big things, but it all matters and has an eternal consequence.

Are you still into your sports?

A Random subject change, but I will go with it. As I said before, I was a health freak but not so much now. Not much time. I've even stopped cycling to work. My dreams of sporting successes were replaced with busyness and chocolate biscuits.

B Well you know the 'Marginal Gains' philosophy employed by sports coaches? The idea that every small act and small change in different places, no matter how seemingly insignificant by itself, when added together will make a huge impact? It leads to athletes improving and gaining wins and victories.

A Yeah, I do. It's like imagining a painting or piece of music. Every individual paint stroke, or note played, is quite insignificant by itself. But when they're all brought together, it can make a masterpiece.

B Well, connecting with someone, loving our neighbour, loving our enemy, is like that. Obviously some acts are bigger and some seem small and insignificant. But all of them are bringing some of God's kingdom to earth. It lays the foundation for the kingdom's ultimate arrival. It all adds up to bringing in more light.

We grow the family by telling people about Jesus and seeing them become Christians.

Which brings the ultimate connection. A relationship with God marked by love, grace and reconciliation. And we foster loving relationships and connect with everyone around us too. Every good, loving, connecting act and action matters.

A
I like the phrase 'growing the family'. It feels like you are trying to give people somewhere to belong, despite everything.

People can look like they have it all sorted. People often think I do, but I don't. I feel so upset and lonely sometimes.

B
This family is for people who don't have it sorted! It's for people looking for real and authentic.

A
You really think this family is for everyone? No matter what they've done in the past or how they see themselves? And despite all of their disconnection and broken relationships? Anyone can join?

B
Anyone can join God's family because it's not about what we've done, but simply about accepting God's unconditional love.[9] Accepting what he did in the life, death and resurrection of Jesus. We're meant to tell people about God and the relationship he offers so they can join the family. His gospel message can change lives.

2 Corinthians 5:14-20

For Christ's love compels us, because we are convinced that one died for all, and therefore all died. And he died for all, that those who live should no longer live for themselves but for him who died for them and was raised again ... All this is from God, who reconciled us to himself through Christ and gave us the ministry of reconciliation: that God was reconciling the world to himself in Christ, not counting people's sins against them. And he has committed to us the message of reconciliation. We are therefore Christ's ambassadors, as though God were making his appeal through us. We implore you on Christ's behalf: be reconciled to God.

John 1:12-13

Yet to all who did receive him, to those who believed in his name, he gave the right to become children of God – children born not of natural descent, nor of human decision or a husband's will, but born of God.

A I really, really like this picture. A loving family that gets bigger as you invite people in, and everyone's welcome.

 And that's why evangelism and telling people about Jesus is important. We want people to know they're no longer alienated from God. They can be brought close and relate to him.[10] We want people to know God has an answer to the relational dysfunction, shame, and loneliness. We want the family to grow.

Matthew 28:18-20

Then Jesus came to them and said, 'All authority in heaven and on earth has been given to me. Therefore go and make disciples of all nations, baptising them in the name of the Father and of the Son and of the Holy Spirit, and teaching them to obey everything I have commanded you. And surely I am with you always, to the very end of the age.'

> I tell people to picture God sitting at a table wanting to share a meal. He wants to chat to you and he's ready to connect. We can get to know him and talk to him, too. Heaven, the kingdom of God, eternal life, getting true life now, is about connecting with God, and his will and desires for us.

John 17:3

Now this is eternal life: that they know you, the only true God, and Jesus Christ, whom you have sent.[11]

A You want to tell people about Jesus? Even if those people don't become Christians in the end? Or even if they take advantage? Or hurt you? Or even if they mock you because of it? Come on, really?

B Yes, yes, yes and yes! We want people to know Jesus, experience a relationship with him and experience the family values.

Yes, we want people to join the family and become Christians, but what they do with the invitation is their choice. All we can do is try to bring in some light despite rejection, mockery and persecution.

That's where we find purpose. We find meaning and authenticity in the life Jesus offers. We tell people about what Jesus did. We love people in small acts like hanging out and not gossiping. And in big acts like sacrificing time and money to help serve in an orphanage. It all brings light into the darkness.

It all adds up. It all matters. It's all marginal gains. The individual notes and paint strokes come together to make a masterpiece. God helps us and works through us to establish his kingdom, the place free from disconnection. People connected to God and each other who then function like a loving family, in this life and for all eternity.

A I was always told to be independent. To be self-reliant. But I feel so lonely sometimes. Like it's all pointless. Doing life, career, etc., all on my own seems like the worst bit most of the time.

B You can become part of the family, you know. You don't have to feel like that. No one is beyond saving. No one is unworthy, because Jesus' cross and resurrection makes us all worthy. Your life matters to him and he wants you to know it matters.

A You mean, you want me to become a Christian, right?

B Is that so bad, based on what we've been chatting about?

Amy, you still there? I hope I haven't said anything wrong.

A You make it all sound so easy, Barney. But there are still things I really don't like about Jesus. I tell you what really does upset me: Christians saying non-Christians will go to hell. There are many people who won't even get the chance to hear about the Christian faith if they live in some remote village somewhere.

Not everyone is able to chat to 'a Barney' or get the chance to hear about the cross. Why should they get punished? I just can't accept that.

B Well, if God is a God of love, I think it's fair to assume that he tries to reach people in multiple ways. Yes, Christians go out and tell people about Jesus, but God also reaches out in dreams. He speaks to people himself.[12] He does lots of things. We can't just reduce him to one thing. People can get to God in different ways.

 A Even if you're right, what about people who say no to the cross? Do they go to hell?

 B Well, 'hell', a place of fire and torture, is ultimately created for the devil to be punished. God is stronger and bigger than the devil, it's not a battle of equals. And more importantly, God is the one in control. God will punish the devil and throw him into the lake of fire, with his demons.

Revelation 20:10

And the devil, who deceived them, was thrown into the lake of burning sulphur, where the beast and the false prophet had been thrown. They will be tormented day and night for ever and ever.

2 Peter 2:4

For if God did not spare angels when they sinned [and became demons], but sent them to hell, putting them in chains of darkness to be held for judgment ...

 A Really? I never knew that. I thought God rules heaven and the devil rules hell. Then from time to time they come to the Earth to battle.

B Most people think that. Most films teach us that. Sometimes even people in church think that! But this isn't the case. Hell is to punish the devil.

Most Christians believe the Bible also teaches that all non-believers are thrown in there too and tortured forever. But some believe it may not mean they're tortured. It may mean that they simply cease to exist. It's like they're destroyed.[13] But ultimately, hell is the opposite of God's kingdom. It's where God isn't. Does that make sense?

A Not really.

B Well, if heaven, God's kingdom, is about God living with his people and being connected, then hell is about being disconnected and not where God is. Whether that is punishment or destruction, it's about being disconnected from God. But Jesus can overcome this eternal disconnection and separation if we choose to turn to him.

Now, I'm not saying that you have to like it. Hell is upsetting and not nice to think about. But it's primarily for the devil to be punished. More importantly, God doesn't delight in it or want people to go there. That's very important.

2 Peter 3:9

The Lord is not slow in keeping his promise, as some understand slowness. Instead he is patient with you, not wanting anyone to perish, but everyone to come to repentance.

Ezekiel 18:23, 27-28

Do I take any pleasure in the death of the wicked? declares the Sovereign LORD. Rather, am I not pleased when they turn from their ways and live? But if a wicked person turns away from the wickedness they have committed and does what is just and right, they will save their life. Because they consider all the offences they have committed and turn away from them, that person will surely live; they will not die.

God is desperate for us to connect. He made the first move by coming to Earth and dying on the cross. But if we reject God's invitation, if we choose not to connect with him and become part of the family, then that's our choice. We will stay disconnected. The invitation is always there, though. We can change our minds.

 A

I kind of see what you mean. If God is love and everything else you said is true, then obviously hell isn't where he wants us to go. And I guess if an authentic, loving relationship requires choice, then we need to choose to relate to God. But I still don't like it. It still makes me angry when I think of it.

B I know. But God really is desperate to get people into the family. He wants all of us to choose him and be with him rather than be separated, because he loves us.

John 3:16-18

For God so loved the world that he gave his one and only Son, that whoever believes in him shall not perish but have eternal life. For God did not send his Son into the world to condemn the world, but to save the world through him. Whoever believes in him is not condemned, but whoever does not believe stands condemned already because they have not believed in the name of God's one and only Son.

Titus 3:4-7

. . . God our Saviour appeared, he saved us, not because of righteous things we had done, but because of his mercy. He saved us through the washing of rebirth and renewal by the Holy Spirit, whom he poured out on us generously through Jesus Christ our Saviour, so that, having been justified by his grace, we might become heirs having the hope of eternal life.

John 10:10

The thief comes only to steal and kill and destroy; I have come that they may have life, and have it to the full.

 A I thought you were only welcomed in or special if you worked for the church. And I couldn't see myself doing that. I like my Sunday lie-ins!

B I've forgotten what they are! But in all seriousness, though, you don't need to work for the church, or have a ground-breaking Christian charity, or do something really 'big' to matter. A person who works in an office and loves his friends and colleagues, and loves God, is used by God to build his kingdom. They bring in light.

Being a generous person, having integrity at work and being a faithful spouse for forty-plus years, even when boredom, greed or selfishness is tempting us, is just as hard and important as the 'big' one-off acts.

A I still don't quite get that. How can someone who works for a church in a big way, who is on stage preaching, be the same as someone who is standing at the door welcoming people, or the person working the PA system, for example? One is clearly bigger and more important than the other one.

B The problem is our society, and even our church culture, ranks certain talents and roles above others. It's all very well saying the preacher is a gifted communicator, but if the PA system wasn't on, no one would hear them. If someone wasn't welcoming and saying hello, people may not even stay to hear the preacher.

Some people work for the church, but many won't. They will be hairdressers, doctors, builders, cleaners, lawyers, stay-at-home parents, etc. But why are some ranked above others? Any one of these people can bring God's light and God's kingdom into their area. It's about how you treat people, how you see people.

It's all marginal gains. Every seemingly small and big act of connection and telling people about the family and loving them matters. Each little and big stroke helps create the beautiful painting. God invites me to help build his kingdom, and it makes my life matter.

A But some people are more important. That's what I've always been told.

B Imagine getting on a plane to go on holiday. The pilot is obviously important, but engineers who passengers never seen are, too. The chef who pre-prepared the meals is important. The air stewards who make sure people are kept safe are vital. Why is it all about the pilot?

A Yes, everyone has their part to play, but the pilot is surely the only one that can't be replaced? I don't want an untrained person just giving it a go!

B Well, I don't know about you, but I wouldn't be happy if the pilot had to fix the engine of the plane. I'd want the trained engineer to do that! Everyone has a role.

A Yeah, all right. But you see what I mean, don't you?

B Yeah, but do you see what I mean? No one needs to feel like a failure or unworthy. God has taken those labels off us and we need to take them off too. We all have our part to play, some roles may get more attention and seem more glamorous, but God works through even the smallest action, using whatever gifts we have.

---

1 Peter 4:10-11
Each of you should use whatever gift you have received to serve others, as faithful stewards of God's grace in its various forms. If anyone speaks, they should do so as one who speaks the very words of God. If anyone serves, they should do so with the strength God provides, so that in all things God may be praised through Jesus Christ. To him be the glory and the power for ever and ever. Amen.

Look, sometimes God calls people to leave what they're doing and do something new. Other times he tells them to stay where they are. Sometimes it seems radical, sometimes it seems simple. But we can live a life which has meaning. We can all be part of growing the family.

We don't need to be on stage to matter.

Matthew 9:9

As Jesus went on from there, he saw a man named Matthew sitting at the tax collector's booth. 'Follow me,' he told him, and Matthew got up and followed him.

Mark 5:18-20

As Jesus was getting into the boat, the man who had been demon-possessed begged to go with him. Jesus did not let him, but said, 'Go home to your own people and tell them how much the Lord has done for you, and how he has had mercy on you.' So the man went away and began to tell in the Decapolis how much Jesus had done for him. And all the people were amazed.

A So you find meaning in playing your part?

B Exactly. Being available, obedient and willing is more important than having ability.

A I just want to find my purpose. I want my life to matter. I thought it was in being famous, or super-unique, or rich. Yet you seem to think it's in how we relate. How we connect with people and the God you believe in. It just feels so different.

B An authentic life is about connection with God, ourselves and others. In the big and small moments. In the dull areas of life and the exciting ones. In the hard and easy times. We just tell people about Jesus and demonstrate the family values.

A Hearing you speak about Christianity seems so different to what I often hear. I always saw it as a test set by a distant, harsh God. You've made my head hurt!

B Ha ha. I'm sure you'll be fine. But I see a God who is very much involved all the time. Like a loving father, building a family. That's what we see the early Church and the first Christians doing. We read about his early followers loving each other, building radical connections and being urged to connect.

Acts 2:44-46

All the believers were together and had everything in common. They sold property and possessions to give to anyone who had need. Every day they continued to meet together in the temple courts. They broke bread in their homes and ate together with glad and sincere hearts . . .

Philippians 2:3-5

Do nothing out of selfish ambition or vain conceit. Rather, in humility value others above yourselves, not looking to your own interests but each of you to the interests of the others. In your relationships with one another, have the same mindset as Christ Jesus . . .

Galatians 5:13-15

You, my brothers and sisters, were called to be free. But do not use your freedom to indulge the flesh; rather, serve one another humbly in love. For the entire law is fulfilled in keeping this one command: 'Love your neighbour as yourself.' If you bite and devour each other, watch out or you will be destroyed by each other.

1 Peter 1:22

Now that you have purified yourselves by obeying the truth so that you have sincere love for each other, love one another deeply, from the heart.

> We're called to connect with everyone. Even those we don't like. Even with those who aren't like us. We find fulfilment in loving and giving ourselves to others. This is where God places value.

Matthew 5:43-44

[Jesus said] You have heard that it was said, 'Love your neighbour and hate your enemy.' But I tell you, love your enemies and pray for those who persecute you . . .

> God can give you the life you crave. Like he did for Toby and Tina. Christ imparts purpose.

> 1: Christians get a new identity and a new kingdom-building purpose.

2: We follow the example of Jesus with the help of the Holy Spirit.

3: We grow the family by telling people about God and his desire to connect and by demonstrating the family values by loving all people.

A Is this where you really ask me to become a Christian, then?

B Would it really be so bad? What's stopping you?

A I just can't, Barney. I am curious, and I admit my life at the moment isn't the one I dreamed of. I really appreciate you talking to me, but I just can't. Not yet.

B Let me stress that the invitation is always there. God will always accept you if you decide to turn to him and accept what Jesus did on the cross, even if you don't fully understand it. But ultimately, only the cross can bring us the deep unconditional loving relationship we all crave. Don't put off this decision.

We can try to find purpose and belonging in money, fame, possessions, looking good, being a 'good Christian', in changing ourselves, in our own strength. But ultimately, only relating to Jesus, a God whose love for us is unconditional and unchanging, will fulfil your need and take away the shame and loneliness.

Make the decision, before the disconnection gets worse, or you get another negative label put on you, or you become numb to the disconnection and think connection is out of your reach.

A Thank you, Barney. I know you really do care. I just need time to process it all. I guess I won't be able to sleep tonight after all!

B I know I've thrown a lot at you. I hope it's helped, even if it's been a bit challenging.

A You have helped me. Thank you.

B Look, I'm delivering another talk on all this connection stuff soon, actually, and I'm going to need to summarise everything I've been speaking to you and others about. I need to get it written down so it's short and to the point. It will explain everything more clearly. I can send you the notes if you want to have a read?

Amy, I need to go, my train is arriving soon. Please, please call me later if you want to chat. Or talk to Toby if you want. But please do something. This invitation is real. God wants to bring you the connection, belonging and authentic life you crave. Your life matters to him, and what you do with it can have eternal consequences.

 I will think about it, and I will read it if you send it, I promise. Have a good evening. And thanks for the chat.

Current status
God, if you're real, then show me I matter.

AUTHOR'S NOTES

Amazingly, things don't just end with the resurrection of Jesus. Believers even receive the Holy Spirit to help us and transform us as we follow the example of Jesus. Our new identity and purpose is rooted in the fact we're in God's family and called to build his kingdom, based on his rule and desires for us. He doesn't need our help to establish his kingdom, but he allows us to join in, and he works through us and gives us meaning. Christ imparts purpose.

Key Takeaways

- As we connect with the designer, we realise what we're designed for.

- Christians get a new identity and a new kingdom-building purpose.

- We follow the example of Jesus with the help of the Holy Spirit.

- We grow the family by telling people about God and his desire to connect and by demonstrating the family values by loving all people.

Real Life Stories

I want to share an incredible story with you. It's a testimony from a woman I used to work with. She had kind of become a Christian and joined a church, but still wasn't sure she totally believed it all.

I remember her saying:

I had a hard life. I had a bad childhood, been a drug addict and never trusted people or ever felt loved.

I ended up getting a job at a Christian charity linked to my church, and everyone was so nice to me. They would ask me how I was, offered to buy me stuff, listened to my rants, forgave me when I lost my temper, helped me when I moved house, talked about God, and would patiently answer my questions.

I remember thinking, what did they want? Why were they doing this? But I realised that they knew God's love, and wanted me to experience it and fully accept it. It was through them that I really got to know who God is.

Not everyone in that story would necessarily know the impact their actions had. There was a chance this woman would have walked away from God, too. Yet these small loving acts from those around her had a massive impact.

Real Life Application

When we pray, when we fast, when we read the Bible together, when we worship, when we serve, we connect with God. When we encourage people, when we use our creative skills to communicate Jesus' message, when we help out at the community meal, when we stop holding grudges at work and try to help our colleagues, when we help at the soup kitchen, when we stop lying but tell the truth, it all drives out disconnection and brings connections and God builds some of his kingdom through us.

Every act is important and valuable to God, and can affect those around us and have eternal consequences.

As we consider what this means for us, it may be worth asking ourselves:

- Does this thought, word, or action create a connection?

- Is it really enough for me to know God sees all the acts of love I do, big or small, and that's all that really matters?

Key Bible Verses

Revelation 21:2-4; Genesis 1:26-28; 2 Corinthians 5:17; Romans 8:11; 38-39; John 13:34-35; Philippians 2:3-5; Matthew 25:34-40; 1 Peter 4:10-11.

Further Reading

Duncan, M., One For All: The Foundations, Oxford: Monarch Books, 2017.

Walton, S., 'The Kingdom of God and the Church', Churchman 129 (Winter 2015), 305-317.

Welby, J., Dethroning Mammon: Making Money Serve Grace, London: Bloomsbury, 2016.

Wright, N.T., 'Imagining the Kingdom: Mission and Theology in Early Christianity', Scottish Journal of Theology 65 (2012), 379-401.

Chapter 4

'Will I always be welcomed?'

Summarising the Connection Model

PART 1

B Hello, I hope you're all having a good week. I need a favour from anyone who needs an excuse to procrastinate!

I'm giving a short talk on the cross and resurrection soon in a church I've not spoken at in a while. I'm trying to succinctly summarise the picture I often use to emphasise one of the things Jesus achieved, but I have less time than usual, and I've said this model so many times now I'm not sure what could be cut and what needs to stay in.

As I've been speaking to all of you about this stuff recently, could you read this and message me back to tell me if it makes sense?

Thanks!

The Connection Model

All views and understandings of the cross need to be biblical. The Bible is where our teaching and revelation comes from. But each wonderful model that has been created over the ages answers a very real and relevant cultural need too, and was crafted in a real human context. We need more than one model and emphasis because different individuals and cultures have different struggles and challenges, and we need to show that all these problems are ultimately answered at the cross of Jesus.

The Connection Model isn't trying to replace other models, or claiming to be the only picture people need to know about now, but it tries to biblically answer a question many people seem to be asking in our churches and in our society nowadays. Namely: *'Can I belong?' instead of 'Have I done wrong?'*

In this model, *sin is defined as disconnection*. It can also be defined as relational dysfunction. Experiencing broken relationships, feeling lonely, separated, unlovable, unworthy and shameful are the effects of sin. People want to overcome this and know someone will love them for who they really are and stick around, first and foremost. God overcoming sin as disconnection is about making a way for us to fully connect and relate in loving relationships with him and others.

The birth and life of Jesus is summarised as *Christ came to connect*:

1: God became human because he wanted to connect with us on our level.

2: God was revealing himself, his inner intimate self, so we could connect with him.

3: Jesus was showing us how to respond to God's love for us and how to love others.

The motivation for the cross is God's love and desire to connect and overcome disconnection. *Love can't be lower than first place.*

In this picture, the death of Jesus is understood mainly through the Bible's teaching on sacrifice and ransom. *The cross and resurrection restores relationships:*

1: It allows us to have the status and fully loving relationship Jesus had with God, we are fully connected with him. He sees our true selves and will never leave us.

2: Past and future disconnection, relational dysfunction and its effects which separate have been dealt with and overcome permanently. These things don't define us or create separation now, they are reversed. Connection is here to stay.

3: We know we're loved, we belong, and are wanted because we are brought into God's loving family, with loving brothers and sisters and a loving father.

The resurrection proves authenticity. It proves that what Jesus said and did leads to life because he was resurrected, is still alive, and has therefore defeated death. His way overcomes the effects of sin and disconnection. Having faith and trusting in him means we can overcome it, too.

This relationship impacts our lives right now, and *Christ imparts purpose*:

1: Christians get a new identity and a new kingdom-building purpose.

2: We follow the example of Jesus with the help of the Holy Spirit.

3: We grow the family by telling people about God and his desire to connect and by demonstrating the family values by loving all people.

As we connect with the designer, we realise what we're designed for. God does not need our help and he can and will ultimately establish his kingdom no matter what. Nevertheless, God chooses to use us and work through us; we get an invitation to be part of building God's kingdom here on Earth. We do this with the help of the Holy Spirit, and every time we relate the way Jesus did, every time we tell someone about Jesus, every time we share and show the family values, God builds some of his kingdom on earth. What we do matters. What we choose to do in our small and big actions has present and eternal consequences.

The gospel shows us that the cross really is like coming home to a family member or dear friend who hugs us and makes us feel valued and loved. We've all experienced and caused disconnection, we need to accept this and trust in Jesus because he has sorted it, and his way leaves us an example for our lives. God never promises that life will be easy afterwards. He may ask us to do things that are hard as we prioritise building his kingdom, and we may still experience the feeling of separation and shame that persist in this world. But we can find hope and answers in Jesus, can be real, be our true self, and know we're always welcomed and part of the family, no matter what. Jesus has done enough. We are connected. We can belong.

PART 2

Toby
Great stuff, Barney!

Tina
This is really good, I think it will help lots of people.

Barney
Glad it sounds OK. Can I ask how you think it helps? It would be good to know.

Toby
It definitely helps me. When I talk to my non-Christian mates about all this stuff, they usually want to hear what I have to say. It seems relevant to where they're at.

Tina
I naturally want to hide away when things go wrong, but you showed me that I need to run towards God when I feel like that. And he will be there ready to welcome me in, no matter what I've done or what the situation is. He has sorted it and wipes the slate clean.

Barney
Thanks, guys. I know it will never answer every question people have, but this is really encouraging.

Tina
It's good that you say life doesn't become perfect too. It feels authentic.

Toby
It really is good, Barney!

Amy
It's interesting. I haven't been able to stop thinking about all this since our chat. Which is annoying!

Toby Do you want to talk about it some more, Amy?

Amy Why not, what have I got to lose?! I'll call you when I get back from work. It may be late, though.

AUTHOR'S NOTES

By now I hope you've caught my vision and heart behind this book. I hope it's brought you closer to God, allowed you to wrestle with ideas, and fall in love with the cross even more, or maybe for the first time.

This Connection Model isn't trying to undermine the other models that explain the multilayered effects of the cross. It's just trying to emphasise gospel and biblical truths and bring them into a coherent framework, so that we feel more confident in our connected relationship with God, and also feel more confident when we talk about him in the culture and context we often find ourselves in.

God wants to have a relationship with you. Overcoming disconnection, broken relationships, shame and unworthiness is part of 'the forgiveness of sins'. God wants you to know you're loved and in the family, and he offers you a fully connected, loving relationship that can lead to the most transforming, authentic and amazing life.

Real Life Application

You may want to listen to the song mentioned on page 154 'In the Family' by Rivers and Robots, and reflect on the words. Or you may want to say the prayer below. Whether you call yourself a Christian or not, please don't just let this book become another idea or interesting read. Let the fully connected, loving relationship God offers us through the birth, life, ministry, death and resurrection of Jesus, become central to our identity, purpose and daily life.

Prayer

Lord Jesus, thank you for what you did on the cross, thank you that your cross deals with all sin, including my sin. Thank you that your forgiveness wipes the slate clean in more ways than I could ever fully appreciate.

I want to say (again) that I put my faith in what you did. I'm sorry for the disconnection I cause, and I want you to meet me in my disconnection and broken relationships. Please send your Holy Spirit, and welcome me into your family and kingdom-building purposes.

God, I'm in.

ENDNOTES

Prologue

'Can I belong?' Instead of 'Have I done wrong?'

1. The belief I have, which states that the cross achieved many things and cannot be reduced to a one-hit wonder, is called the Kaleidoscopic View. This idea states that the outcomes and impact of the life, death, and resurrection of Jesus are so huge and so varied, no single model, picture, or understanding can fully summarise or do justice to what Jesus achieved. Therefore, we need to use multiple metaphors and pictures to communicate the cross to those around us. Joel Green, a New Testament scholar, argues that the Bible never gives a single interpretation to explain the cross, so we shouldn't try to do so. He also says that there is no need to try to make one understanding more important than the others, and they are all needed to articulate the importance and relevance of the cross in the modern world. The French evangelical theologian Henri Blocher would also say that all the different biblical pictures complement each other and don't undermine each other, and actually make Jesus' death and resurrection fuller and richer. The Former Archbishop of Canterbury Rowan Williams notes that 'The cross, you could say, doesn't stand still. Our understanding, our absorption of its meaning, is always a living process in which one image, one category, again and again moves us into another'. The Baptist minister Stephen Homes agrees that the Bible doesn't limit itself to one image or idea, so believers cannot just share one image or idea either. Professor Stephen Finlan points out that Paul the Apostle often uses more than one metaphor to interpret another and combines multiple explanations. For example: Jesus paid the price for the believer's freedom (Ransom Model), by his blood (Sacrificial and/or Martyr Model), and died in the believer's place (Penal Substitution). I also think it's helpful to remember that Paul used different approaches and emphasised different aspects when talking about the cross and resurrection, depending on his context and audience. This doesn't mean

that Paul changed or distorted the heart of the gospel message to make it more appealing (1 Corinthians 2:1-2; Galatians 1:6-12; Colossians 2:6-8; 1 Thessalonians 2:1-7). It means that he communicated the truth in a relevant way to his listeners. For example, in Acts 17 Paul used the Scriptures to reason and preach to the Jews in their synagogues (Acts 17:1-4,10-12). Yet in the same chapter, it says Paul used an altar 'To an unknown God' to preach to the Greeks and philosophers in Athens (Acts 17:16-34). These groups of people had very different starting points with different understandings and beliefs, which is why I believe Paul emphasised different aspects of the truth to meet these people where they were at, in order to tell them about Jesus' death and resurrection. We can therefore use different biblical pictures, models, and emphasis to explain what Jesus achieved. See Beilby, J., and Eddy, P.R. (eds.), *The Nature of the Atonement: Four Views,* Downers Grove: IVP, 2006, 64, 157. See also Blocher, H., 'Biblical Metaphors and the Doctrine of Atonement', *JETS* 47/4 (December 2004), 629-645, esp. 629, 645. See also Finlan, S., *Problems with the Atonement: The Origins of, and Controversy About, the Atonement Doctrine,* Collegeville, MN: Liturgical Press, 2005, 58-59. See also Holmes, S.R., *The Wondrous Cross: Atonement and Penal Substitution in The Bible and History:* London: Paternoster, 2007, 7-9. See also Johnson, A.J., *Atonement: A Guide for the Perplexed*, London: Bloomsbury, 2015, 1-8. See also Williams, R., *God With Us: The Meaning of the Cross and Resurrection. Then and Now,* London: SPCK, 2017, 54-55.

2. We must remember that the context the cross and resurrection is preached in cannot be where the *meaning* of the cross is found. In other words, we need to remember that the Bible reveals the meaning and objective truth of Jesus' death and resurrection. Our context only helps us to decide which picture or emphasis is most relevant and applicable to those who are listening. See Handern, C., 'The Atonement: The Kaleidoscopic View', *Born of the World* website 24 June 2009, http://bornoftheword.blogspot.co.uk/2009/06/atonement-kaleidoscopic-view.html (accessed 26.2.18). See also endnote 1 from this chapter.

3. Different biblical models and pictures help us to understand the different things Jesus achieved on the cross, and how these different achievements can overcome the problems people face in different contexts. For example:

The Christus Victor Model teaches that Jesus' life, death, and resurrection defeated Satan and the evil powers that cause suffering. Jesus is the victor and has won the spiritual battle and defeated sin. This model was developed in the early centuries after Jesus' death in a culture and context where spiritual fear reigned, and most Christians suffered persecution, captivity, slavery and economic pressure. People had a profound awareness and experience of evil, and suffering was part of life. It's no surprise that the Swedish theologian Gustav Aulèn (who actually gave it the name 'Christus Victor') could give this model fresh attention in the 1930s when Europe had been experiencing war, death and the rise of dictators and oppressive ideologies. The Christus Victor Model is the most helpful and relevant in these contexts because it acknowledges sin as evil and suffering, the spiritual powers behind it, and shows people that Jesus ultimately overcomes it and frees believers through his death on the cross. See Pugh, B., *Atonement Theories: A Way Through the Maze*, Eugene, OR: Cascade, 2014, 1-3, 8-9. See also Schmiechen, P., *Saving Power: Theories of Atonement and Forms of the Church*, Grand Rapids, MI: Eerdmans, 2005, 123-130.

The Satisfaction Model teaches that the cross restores God's honour and pays the debt humanity owed to him. Anselm, the Archbishop of Canterbury from 1093 to 1109, came up with this model and it's a great example of contextual theology. In his context and culture, society believed that it was important to uphold people's honour and they needed to restore someone's honour if they insulted it. Anselm argued that when people sin they insulted God's honour, so they needed to restore it. However, humanity sinned so much and their debt was so large that only God could was able to fully pay it off, but humanity needed to pay it because the debt belonged to them. This is why Jesus, who is fully God and fully human, died on the cross: Jesus is God because only God could pay the huge debt, and he is human because the debt needed to be paid by humanity. This means Jesus' death and resurrection dealt with sin and resulted with God's honour being restored and humanity being made debt-free. Anselm's biblical picture didn't explain every aspect of the cross, but it spoke directly and relevantly to people in his context, and showed them how the cross overcomes their problem. See Saint Anselm, *Cur Deus Homo? To Which is Added a Selection from His Letters*, Edinburgh: John Grant, 1909, 25. See also McDonald, H.D., *The Atonement of the Death of Christ: In Faith, Revelation, and History*,

Grand Rapids, MI: Baker, 1985, 163-167. See also Whittock, M., and Whittock, E., *Christ: The First 2000 Years*, Oxford: Lion, 136-137.

The Liberation Model teaches that the cross hasn't just dealt with the believer's personal sin, but helps liberate them and others from oppressive social structures, too. For example, James Cone was part of the civil rights movement in America in the 1960s. Cone taught that Christianity has no room for racism and he hated seeing black people oppressed in his context. Therefore, he developed the Black Liberation Model because people around him were seeking liberation from oppressive racism. It was the most helpful and relevant way to show people in his context how the cross helps and overcomes their problem. See Schmiechen, P., *Saving Power: Theories of Atonement and Forms of the Church*, 141-145. See also Antonio, E., 'Black Theology', in Rowland, C. (ed.), *The Cambridge Companion to Liberation Theology*, Cambridge: CUP, 1999, 63-88, esp. 63-65.

4. The Penal Substitution Model places sin, and the death and resurrection of Jesus, into a very legal framework. It teaches that sin occurs when people break God's good, just and holy law. Everyone is judged 'guilty' because we all break some of God's law, and therefore commit sin, and should therefore be punished. However, God in his love sent Jesus, who was our substitute in that he died in the sinner's place even though he was sinless, and took the punishment the just law of God demands. Jesus suffered instead of the believer. His death and resurrection dealt with sin, frees us and declares us 'not guilty'. Interestingly, many evangelical Protestant Christian today think the Penal Substitution Model is the main/only way to understand the cross and resurrection of Jesus. However, most Christians didn't interpret sin and the cross like this until after 1215, when King John was made to sign a document known as the Magna Carta. This stated that there is a set of just laws that everyone, including the king, the most powerful person in the land, must follow. People who break them must be punished. After this big historical and political shift, many Christians and theologians' explanation of sin focused on humanity's failure to abide by God's just law. A law that's so holy and right that even God, the most powerful being in the universe, has to stick to and must decide to punish us because we break it. This cultural shift and understanding was so ingrained in many (European) cultures after the Magna Carta was signed, along with the

rise of the legal system in European societies, that by the time Reformers like Martin Luther and John Calvin started to teach in the sixteenth century, it was 'natural' and 'obvious' to view sin as breaking God's law. For Luther, the law itself is what we need saving from. Not God, or the devil, or corruption, but the law's demand for punishment. John Calvin had a more positive view of the law, and later argued that God must uphold the law because it's good and just but he himself takes the punishment on the cross to save believers. All of this demonstrates that this model arose out of a specific context to relevantly answer people's needs and problems, and used ideas and concepts that the surrounding culture could relate to and understand. Therefore, if people around us are asking different questions and have different problems, then maybe a different biblical picture can arise to answer the question and needs of today. This would be following in the footsteps of other great Christian thinkers from the past. See Holmes, S.R., *The Wondrous Cross*, 60-63. See also Pugh, B., *Atonement Theories: A Way Through the Maze*, 63-64, 70-71, 75. See also Schmiechen, P., *Saving Power: Theories of Atonement and Forms of the Church*, 104. See also Blocher, H.A.G., 'Sin', in Alexander, T.D., and Rosner, B.S. (eds.), *New Dictionary of Biblical Theology*, Leicester: IVP, 2006, 781-788, esp. 783. See also Grudem, W., *Systematic Theology: An Introduction to Biblical Doctrine*, Nottingham: IVP, 2011, 490. See also endnote 3 from this chapter.

5. Many Christians teach that the motivation for the cross is love, and sin can be understood, at least to some extent, as broken relationships. The cross and resurrection overcomes this problem of broken relationships and reconciles us with a loving God, who brings us into his family, and allows us to have loving relationships with others too. See Bray, G., *God Has Spoken: A History of Christian Theology*, Wheaton, IL: Crossway, 2014, 88. See also Flood, D., 'A Relational Understanding of Atonement', in Montgomery, B., Oord, T.J., and Winslow, K.S. (eds.), *Relational Theology: A Contemporary Introduction*, Eugene, OR: Wipf & Stock, 2012, 40-42. See also Jersak, B., *A More Christlike God: A More Beautiful Gospel*, Pasadena, CA: CWR Press, 2015, 19, 21-22, 47. See also Keller, T., *Making Sense of God: An Invitation to the Sceptical*, London: Hodder & Stoughton, 2016, 118, 125-126, 247-254. See also Lane, S.T., and Tripp, P.D., *Relationships: A Mess Worth Making*, Canada: New Growth Press, 2008, 1-2. See also Macleod, D., *Christ Crucified: Understanding*

the Atonement, Nottingham: IVP, 2014, 151-155, 161-162. See also Schmiechen, P., *Saving Power: Theories of Atonement and Forms of the Church*, 288-297. See also Scott, J.M., *Adoption as Sons of God: An Exegetical Investigation into the Background of UIOQESI/A in the Pauline Corpus*, Tübingen: Mohr, 1992, 174, 261. See also Smail, T., *Like Father, Like Son: The Trinity Imaged in Our Humanity*, Milton Keynes: Paternoster Press, 2005, 153-156, 200. See also Whittock, M., and Whittock, E., *Christ: The First 2000 Years*, 136-138. See also Williams, R., *God With Us: The Meaning of the Cross and Resurrection. Then and Now*, 8-10, 66-67. See also Yoder, J.H., *Preface to Theology: Christology and Theological Method*, Grand Rapids, MI: Brazon Press, 2002, 287.

Chapter 1

'How do I talk about sin?'

Christ came to connect

1. The latest research suggests that loneliness is on the rise in Great Britain. For example, almost 45 per cent of UK adults say they feel lonely at least some of the time, and 18 per cent say they feel lonely often or all of the time. Sadly, 12 per cent said they rarely feel loved, and 5 per cent said that they never feel loved. 13 per cent of UK adults say that they don't have a close friend or someone to rely on in a personal crisis. Research also suggests that loneliness in the UK peaks at two points, namely in those aged twenty-five years and under, and in those aged over sixty-five. The Get Connected helpline, which is for people under twenty-five, receives calls from over 3,500 young people each year. In addition, 65 per cent of sixteen to twenty-four-year-olds report feeling lonely some of the time, and 32 per cent say it's often or always. Of the over sixty-five-year-olds, 10 per cent say they are often or always lonely, while 41 per cent say their pet or TV is their main source of company. 50 per cent of disabled people will feel lonely on any given day. (These statistics were taken from the following websites in January 2018, and were accurate on this date: ageuk.org.uk, campaigntoendloneliness.org, jocoxloneliness.org, relate.org.uk.)

2. Genesis 1 and 2 contain two creation narratives that record God creating humans and the universe. These chapters are really important because they show us what the world was like prior to sin entering it in Genesis 3. So the story of Adam and Eve shows us God's original intention for all humanity and his intention for our relational dynamics, romantic or otherwise. We read that Adam is described as being lonely and God himself says this is 'not good' (Genesis 2:18). No animal can rectify this situation either (Genesis 2:20). So God created Eve (Genesis 2:21-22). This shows that a relationship with another person was essential before God's creation was 'good'. As Alistair McFadyen, a lecturer in theology, puts it, 'Adam and Eve become human only in relation to each other [and in] dialogical encounter'. This is echoed by Genesis 1:27, which says 'So God created mankind in his own image, in the image of God he created them; male and female he created them.' In this verse man and woman are being made simultaneously, which again points to the idea that people need to live and work together, to exist in plurality and not in isolation. This is supported in Genesis 2:25 when it says that Adam and Eve felt 'no shame' between them. All of this emphasises that God designed people to be in good relationships with each other, which are meant to be free from shame and there should be no barriers between people. This idea is supported more by the fact that when sin enters the first human relationship, Adam and Eve cover themselves up and hide from God (Genesis 3:7-8), meaning a relationship without sin really should have no barriers and no need for withdrawal. As Max Turner, the evangelical British New Testament Scholar, says, Genesis 1 and 2 teaches that people need relationships to fulfil their godly purpose and personhood. See Fretheim, T.E., *God and World in the Old Testament: A Relational Theology of Creation,* Nashville, TN: Abingdon, 2005, 56. See also Klein, W.W., Blomberg, C.L., and Hubbard Jr., R.L., *Introduction to Biblical Interpretation,* Revised Edition, Nashville, TN: Thomas Nelson, 2004, 493. See also McFadyen, A.I., *The Call to Personhood: A Christian Theory of the Individual in Social Relationships,* Cambridge: CUP, 1990, 32. See also Smail, T., *Like Father, Like Son: The Trinity Imaged in Our Humanity,* 51-52. See also Turner, M., 'The Challenge of Personhood: Towards a Theology of Personhood', in London Bible College Authors, *Christian Life and Today's World: Not Conformed but Transformed,* Bletchley: Scripture Union, 2002, 47-63, esp. 57, 60. See also Von Rad, G., *Genesis,* The Old Testament Library, London: SCM, 1961, 83.

3. The biblical understanding of sin includes many elements and it cannot just be reduced to one thing. Having said that, one of the main emphasis/definitions of sin that gains lots of attention today is that sin is disobedience. Sin happens when we break God's law. Many theologians and Christian authors, such as Gerald Bray, would say sin is primarily about breaking God's law and this causes a sinful state that leads to broken relationships. Timothy Lane and Paul Tripp, both of whom are Christian counsellors and church leaders, would also define sin as primarily not living under God's rule, and individuals deciding to become their own ruler. This disobedience causes people to be self-centred and think about themselves. However, on the other hand, many have adopted another emphasis/definition as the primary understanding of sin, which teaches that sin is a distorted or broken relationship with God. In other words, individuals and humanity take their eyes off God and don't relate to him properly, and we disconnect from God, then we disobey him. In this understanding of sin, disobedience is seen as a consequence and not the cause. Michael Lodahl, a theologian in the Church of the Nazarene, would argue sin is anything short of loving God and neighbour, which Jesus said is the greatest commandment. Being free from sin means believers can live relationally in love to God and others. Augustine of Hippo, the very influential Christian theologian who lived AD 354-430, believed sin is primarily about people falling away from God and not looking to him or relating properly to him. Others would build on this and see sin as the distortion of the relationship between us as personal beings and our personal creator God, and a distortion of the relationship happens when we try to be like God and take his place. This is seen in Genesis 11:1-9, for example, when the people try to build the tower of Babel, and in Genesis 3:1-5 when Adam and Eve eat the fruit in order to be like God. These people weren't relating to God properly and it's these distorted relationships with God that are the main problem. It's therefore legitimate to argue that sin can be seen as disconnection, and people turning away from wanting a loving God in their lives, disregarding God and relating unlovingly. They sin when they break the relationships and this affects the individual and other people as well. (However, I want to stress again that sin has many elements to it and one emphasis/definition can't give the full picture. All the different biblical definitions should be seen as part of a complex Christian understanding that encompasses different truths, but I do think specific elements can

be emphasised at different points and in different contexts.) See Bray, G., *God Has Spoken: A History of Christian Theology*, 84, 88. See also Gunton, C.E., *The Christian Faith: An Introduction to Christian Doctrine,* Oxford: Blackwell Publishing, 2008, 59-63. See also Lane, S.T., and Tripp, P.D., *Relationships: A Mess Worth Making*, 32-33, 35. See also MacCulloch, D., *A History of Christianity: The First Thousand Years,* London: Penguin Books, 2010, 305. See also Lodahl, M., 'Sin In Relational Perspective' in Montgomery, B., Oord, T.J., and Winslow, K. (eds.), *Relational Theology: A Contemporary Introduction*, 37-39, esp. 37-39.

4. The idea that sin can be defined as relational dysfunction is supported by work of French evangelical Blocher, who points out that when the Old and New Testament are read in their original languages, there is more than one word for 'sin'. The variety in the vocabulary shows the authors of the Bible understood sin in more than one way. For example, some words for sin communicate the idea of 'missing the mark' or 'falling short' of the desired goal (e.g. Proverbs 8:36). While other words for sin communicate the idea of being ungodly and facing condemnation in court (e.g. Deuteronomy 25:1), while other words communicate the idea of falling by the way side and falling away (e.g. Hebrews 6:6). These are just a few examples. Nevertheless, when taken as a whole, the Bible's vocabulary for sin shows us that the idea of disruption to inter-personal relationships and failure to meet acceptable standards is there. This concept is given more support when Kenneth Bailey, the author and lecturer in Middle Eastern New Testament studies, and his work on the Lord's Prayer is examined. He points out that in Matthew 6:12, Jesus teaches his follower to pray 'And forgive us our debts, as we have also forgiven our debtors.' This is paralleled in Luke 11:4, but interestingly, Luke uses the words 'debts and sins'. In Matthew and Luke, debts refer to unfulfilled obligations towards God and other people. In other words, the things people failed to do, like when they failed to help or reach out in compassion or be a good friend. The word 'sin' in Luke's passage means the unloving acts people commit towards each other, like murder. This double meaning is given more weight when we remember that Jesus would have been speaking Aramaic. The Aramaic word '*khoba*' would have carried the idea of both debt and sin, so Jesus' words would have been less defined and encompassed both definitions. So the believer is taught by Jesus to pray for forgiveness for the loving

acts they fail to do, and the unloving acts they do. Furthermore, asking for forgiveness is preceded by the request for God to give believers their daily bread (Matthew 6:11; Luke 11:3). This part of the prayer stresses that forgiveness is an ongoing daily need, and is linked strongly to community and relationship because people cannot live together and build community and relationship unless they continually seek God's forgiveness and forgive each other. All of this gives weight to the idea that sin can be understood as relational dysfunction, not exclusively, but nevertheless a very relational definition is valid. See Bailey, K.E., *Jesus Through Middle Eastern Eyes: Cultural Studies in the Gospels*, London: SPCK, 2008, 125-126. See also Blocher, H.A.G., 'Sin', in Alexander, T.D., and Rosner, B.S. (eds.), *New Dictionary of Biblical Theology*, 781-788, esp. 782-783.

5. The Ten Commandments are found in Exodus 20:1-17. One way to categorise them is to say that the first four commandments teach us how to relate lovingly towards God. So we shouldn't make idols to worship, and we should make time for God on the Sabbath, for example. The other six commandments then teach us how to relate lovingly towards our neighbour. So we shouldn't lie, commit adultery, steal, or murder. We shouldn't even covert or get jealous of other people's possessions, meaning thoughts and actions are both important.

6. Idolatry is warned against a lot in the Bible (e.g. Exodus 23:13; Leviticus 17:7; Deuteronomy 4:15-19; Jeremiah 1:16; 51:17; Ezekiel 14:1-6).

7. God always showed his faithfulness to his people. Even though they worshipped other gods, didn't listen to his instructions or keep their promises to him, he ultimately remained faithful and tried to bring them back into a relationship with himself (e.g. Exodus 20:24; Jeremiah 26:2-3,13,19; 29:10-14; Malachi 3:5-7).

8. In the Old Testament, the consequences of some sins led to people being 'cut off' from the community. They were separated because they went against God's instruction willingly and knowingly, with an arrogance and distain for want God wanted. For example, Numbers 15:30 says 'But anyone who sins defiantly, whether native-born or foreigner, utters blasphemy against the LORD and must be cut off from

the people of Israel. Because they have despised the LORD's word and broken his commands, they must surely be cut off; their guilt remains on them' (see also Exodus 12:19; 31:14; Leviticus 7:25-27; 19:8; Number 9:13, 20). God had given his people a way to establish a relationship with him, when they rejected that relationship they were intentionally treating it with contempt. Consequently, these people were removed from community and their sin broke their relationship with God and others. In fact, sin often has a very communal element to it in the Old Testament because it not only affected the individual, but the whole community, who often had to respond and deal with the consequences of the individual who sinned (Deuteronomy 21:1-9; Judges 20:4-11; Joshua 7:1-13). See Ashley, T.R., *The Book of Numbers,* The New International Commentary on the Old Testament, Grand Rapids, MI: Eerdmans, 1993, 288-289. See also Budd, P.J., *Numbers,* Word Biblical Commentary, Volume 5, Waco, TX: Word Books, 1984, 98, 174. See also Grudem, W., *Systematic Theology: An Introduction to Biblical Doctrine,* 503. See also Woudstra, M.H., *The Book of Joshua,* The New International Commentary on the Old Testament, Grand Rapids, MI: Eerdmans, 1981, 38-39.

9. Gaining eternal life is about more than just living forever. Jesus is the pioneer of true life and brings life to God's people (John 6:68; Acts 3:15; 2 Timothy 1:10). In the life he brings there is fellowship with the Creator (John 17:3) and other believers (1 Thessalonians 4:13-18; Revelation 6:9-11; 15:2). This 'eternal life' will be fully gained in eternity, but it's also partly experienced and lived out immediately on this earth. Those living in 'eternal life' stand in the a place of blessing right now, and get to experience a relationship with God and others which reflects the ones seen in Genesis 1 and 2 before sin entered the world. John 10:10 is about God offering us an existence where there is no sin or separation between us and himself, where his purposes are unhindered, and where relationships are fully connected and truly fulfilling. This life can start now, even though the believer will experience it in full and forever for eternity, which is where the living forever aspect comes in. See Johnson, D.H., 'Life' in Alexander, T.D., and Rosner, B.S. (eds.), *New Dictionary of Biblical Theology,* 640-644, esp. 642, 644. See also endnote 11 from chapter 3.

10. Jesus' birth, life, and ministry are often forgotten in the shadow of the cross and resurrection in books and preaches. It's true that without the cross and resurrection Christians aren't saved, and this was the event which changed everything. It's the very thing that shapes Christians' understanding of God and how we're saved (1 Corinthians 1:22-24), and is therefore rightly the focus. However, if people only had to know about his cross and resurrection, then the Gospel writers wouldn't have recorded the events of Jesus' birth, life and ministry. It's important to know that without these events Christians aren't saved either, because Jesus had to live an authentic human life to truly save humanity (Galatians 4:4-5; Hebrews 2:14-18). He wasn't just transported down from heaven as a thirty-year-old that got lead to Pontius Pilate and condemned to die straight away. He was born and grew up like any other human. Pictures and models for understanding Jesus' death often reduce the importance of his life. For example, critics of Anselm's Satisfaction Model note that he falls into this trap. We must realise that without Jesus' birth, life, ministry, death, resurrection and ascension, we cannot be saved. See Quash, B., and Ward, M. (eds.), *Heresies and How to Avoid Them: Why it Matters What Christians Believe,* London: SPCK, 2007, 15-69. See also Letham, R., *The Holy Trinity: In Scripture, History, Theology, and Worship,* Phillipsburg, NJ: P&R, 2004, 24-69. See also Whittock, M., and Whittock, E., *Christ: The First 2000 Years*, 136-137.

11. Jesus is fully God and fully human at the same time, and not just some strange mix of the two. The New Testament authors and the first followers of Christ believed deeply that Jesus was their Saviour, and he was both fully human and fully God. Over time, the Church developed this idea and outlined what this means. For example, the biblical teaching and the Church states that Jesus has always been the fully eternal God and was never created (Hebrews 1:3; Colossians 1:19). He is also a real human, and wasn't just walking around on Earth as God 'dressed up' or 'disguised' to look like a human (John 1:14; Philippians 2:7). He didn't have a split personality either, where one body was home to both a 'god personality' and a 'human personality'. Jesus is fully God and fully human at the same time. See Letham, R., *The Holy Trinity: In Scripture, History, Theology, and Worship,* 15-69. See also Quash, B., and Ward, M. (eds.), *Heresies and How to Avoid Them: Why it Matters What Christians*

Believe, 15-69. See also Tomlin, G., *The Widening Circle: Priesthood as God's Way of Blessing the World*, London: SPCK, 2014, 22-24. See also Whittock, M., and Whittock, E., *Christ: The First 2000 Years*, 26-39.

12. The Prodigal Son story is found in Luke 15:11-32. The story where Jesus meets the woman at the well is found in John 4:1-42. The story about Zacchaeus is found in Luke 19:1-9.

13. The account of Jesus turning the tables over in the synagogue is found in Matthew 21:12-17.

Chapter 2

'Am I loved?'

The cross and resurrection restores relationships

1. Jesus willingly died on the cross. In Mark 10:45 he says that he 'did not come to be served, but to serve, and to give his life as a ransom for many'. He *gave* his life. He also proclaims in John 10:15-18 that '. . . I lay down my life for the sheep . . . No one takes it from me, but I lay it down of my own accord. I have authority to lay it down and authority to take it up again. This command I received from my Father'. Yes he was obedient to the Father, but he chose to be obedient and sacrifice his life. (See also John 15:13; John 19:8-11.) It wasn't easy, enjoyable, or simple, but he chose to do it to save humanity.

2. The Trinity is one of those things that cannot be fully explained. There is a mystery surrounding it. However, believers aren't left completely in the dark. The Bible and Church history professes that God is one, Christians believe in one God. Yet God has three distinct persons: God the Father, God the Son, and God the Holy Spirit. Importantly, they are all distinct, one being does not 'transform' into the Son, then into the Father, etc. So they are distinct but all God, and all one God. Therefore,

because Jesus is God and came down to Earth as a human, through God the Son God *suffered as a human* on the cross. In other words, because there is only one God, God himself acted to save us and paid the price when he died on the cross as the sinless human (2 Corinthians 5:19; Philippians 2:5-8; Colossians 1:19-20; Hebrews 1:1-4). God willingly suffered as a human adult, and not as an unwilling child. See Ward, M., 'Theopaschitism: Is Jesus Christ Able or Unable to Suffer In His Divine Nature?', in Quash, B., and Ward, M. (eds.), *Heresies and How to Avoid Them: Why it Matters What Christians Believe*, 59-69, esp. 59, 67-69. See also Macleod, D., *Christ Crucified: Understanding the Atonement*, 156.

3. It's worth me saying that forgiving someone isn't the same as being a doormat. Sometimes, we can forgive someone and build a stronger relationship and connection afterwards, but sometimes the dynamic of the relationship will need to change. We may forgive someone but need to keep our distance, or stop them from having the same influence and power in our lives, so that we don't get hurt again. For example, if a spouse leaves a marriage after domestic abuse, or a toxic manipulative 'friendship' is ended, forgiveness allows that person to (slowly) stop letting the pain affect them, and trust God in that situation, and even wish the best for the person they forgive. However, it doesn't mean the relationship can go back to what it was. Forgiveness doesn't always mean acting like nothing happened. It can mean putting boundaries in place to avoid it happening again. We should also never underestimate how hard giving forgiveness is for some people in some situations. It's rarely quick and is often a process. God asks believers to forgive others and it is something we must learn to do and keep doing, but we need to remember it's not always easy, or something we need to do in our own strength without God's help.

4. Before God commanded his followers to make sacrifices, Noah does it when he leaves the ark (Genesis 8:20). Cain and Abel each make one before Noah did (Genesis 4:2-4). This shows us that sacrifices are a normal and natural thing for them to do. See Holmes, S.R., *The Wondrous Cross*, 17-23.

5. Sacrifice is clearly an important part of the relationship between God and his people in the Old Testament, mainly because it dealt with the

problem of sin. John Hartley, a professor of Old Testament Studies, points out that the book of Leviticus talks extensively about sacrifices. He says we need to realise it's more than just a book of rules, though, because it revealed the way to maintain a connection with a God who is holy, other and all-powerful. Leviticus teaches that sin puts the relationship of the sinner and God in jeopardy, but God gave his people the sacrificial system and laws because it brought forgiveness of sin, meaning strained relationships could be restored and the personal God could have close fellowship with his people. The Baptist minister Stephen Homes would agree that the sacrifices brought forgiveness (Leviticus 4-6; 14:20), and would add that they brought peace and well-being too (Leviticus 3; 7:11-12), and they also pleased God (Leviticus 1:9,13,17). The sacrificial system, which plays a key role in the Old Testament and not just in the book of Leviticus, meant that people could overcome the separation and disconnection of sin and experience closeness and fellowship with God. This is demonstrated in Exodus 20:24 which says 'Make an altar of earth for me and sacrifice on it your burnt offerings and fellowship offerings, your sheep and goats and your cattle. Wherever I cause my name to be honoured, *I will come to you* and bless you'. Rowan Williams, the retired Archbishop of Canterbury, says that the sacrifice covers over the sin and disorder of the individual and/or community and removes sin's consequences. The gift of the sacrifice turned away God's anger and displeasure, and brought God back into an active relationship. Brent Peterson, a pastor and professor, agrees that God gave his people a way to be reconciled and restore relationships through the embodied worship of the sacrificial system. However, the outward worship without inward repentance meant nothing (Leviticus 1:4-9; 4:3-13). The fact that God was interested in the internal motives and the heart of the person making the sacrifice, stresses the importance of genuine relational connection over just following external rules. All of this demonstrates to us that firstly, sacrifice was clearly an important part of creating and maintaining the relationship between God and his people. Secondly, it shows that God created the sacrificial system as a way for his people to gain forgiveness of sins, because he *wanted* to relate and be present with them. See Hartley, J.E., *Leviticus*, Word Biblical Commentary, Volume 4, Dallas, TX: Word Books, 1992, lvi, lxxi, lxxii, 276. See also Holmes, S.R., *The Wondrous Cross*, 20-21. See also Peterson, B.D., 'Worship as Relational Renewal and Redemption of the World', in Montgomery, B.,

Oord, T. J., and Winslow, K. (eds.), *Relational Theology: A Contemporary Introduction*, 76-79, esp. 77-78. See also Williams, R., *God With Us: The Meaning of the Cross and Resurrection. Then and Now*, 24-25.

6. Making sacrifices to God wouldn't be acceptable or pleasing to him if those making the sacrifice were creating unloving and distorted relationships with people around them (e.g. Proverbs 14:31; 21:3; Jeremiah 6:19-20; Amos 5:21-24; Micah 6:6-8).

7. Leviticus 16 shows that the Day of Atonement, also called Yom Kippur, was a very important day in the Jewish calendar. It was the most holy day, in fact. This is because it allowed God's people to receive forgiveness, overcome sin and maintain their relationship with God and others in the community (Leviticus 16:29-34). On the Day of Atonement two goats were chosen, and the first one was sacrificed as a sin offering (Leviticus 16:9,15-16). This happened so that the sins of the people could be forgiven. The second goat, called the scapegoat, had the hands of the priest placed on it as he confessed all the sins, iniquities and rebellions of God's people. This happened so that the sins of the people could be symbolically 'transferred' to the innocent goat, which was then led away from the community and driven into the wilderness to die as it carried away the sins of the people (Leviticus 16:10,20-22). Importantly, in the New Testament, Hebrews 10:1-18 teaches us that Jesus' sacrifice deals with sin and removes it forever. He can achieve this because unlike the animal sacrifices that only dealt with sin temporarily (Hebrews 10:3-4), Jesus' perfect sacrifice was final and all-sufficient (Hebrews 10:10,14). Jesus therefore becomes our sacrificed goat and scapegoat, that permanently removes sin from us, so that we can fully relate to God and others again. See Mathews, K.A., *Leviticus: Holy God, Holy People,* Preaching The Word, Wheaton, IL: Crossway, 2009, 134-135, 137-139. See also Hartley, J.E., *Leviticus*, Word Biblical Commentary, Volume 4, 241. See also Gerstenberger, E.S., *Leviticus: A Commentary*, The Old Testament Library, Louisville, KY: Westminster John Knox Press, 1996, 211, 231.

8. In Exodus 29:38-42 God commanded that two lambs were sacrificed daily, so that he could meet and connect with his people every day. Exodus 12:1-13 records the passage about the Passover lamb.

9. Leviticus 17:11 states that the blood of the sacrificed animal is what made the sacrifice work, and the blood reversed the problems and effects of sin. Now, the blood didn't *possess* magic powers or a spiritual life force, rather, it *represented* the life of the animal. To put it another way, I could say that if all the blood is lost from the body the result is death, meaning blood is needed for life. So when the blood was shed by an animal as a sacrifice before God in the way he instructed, that life which the blood represents was surrendered. This surrendered life could then cover up sin, meaning the sin was dealt with, and life and holiness was restored to the people. We see this demonstrated in Leviticus 4:3-7, where the priest would spread the blood of the unblemished sacrificed animal in the tent and on the altar to cover up sin, bring forgiveness and restore holiness. (See also Leviticus 14:48-53.) See Mathews, K.A., *Leviticus: Holy People, Holy God*, Preaching The Word, 44-45, 149-150. See also Hartley, J.E., *Leviticus*, Word Biblical Commentary, Volume 4, 273-277.

10. Interestingly, the Bible never explicitly teaches that Jesus' death was a ransom paid to God or Satan. Jesus said he would give his life as a ransom (Mark 10:45; Matthew 20:28) and Paul the Apostle wrote about Jesus' death in this way too (e.g. 1 Timothy 2:6), yet the Bible never makes it clear who this ransom was paid to. In the third century, Origen was the first Church Father to explicitly teach that the ransom was paid to Satan. He taught that God did this to deceive Satan because Satan had legitimate rights over humanity and we needed to be freed. Many in the Church accepted this idea until Anselm, a key theologian, refuted it in the eleventh century. Anselm argued that the ransom was paid to God and Satan had no legitimate claims over humanity. The lack of clarity in the Bible about who the ransom was paid to means the matter is still open for debate. Nevertheless, the Bible makes it clear that Jesus' death was a ransom. See Morris, L., 'Redemption', in Hawthorne, G.F., Martin, R.P., and Reid, D.G. (eds.), *Dictionary of Paul and His Letters*, Leicester: IVP, 1993, 784-786, esp. 785. See also Schmiechen, P., *Saving Power: Theories of Atonement and Forms of the Church*, 25, 31, 36, 55. See also Pugh, B., *Atonement Theories: A Way Through the Maze*, 2014, 5-8.

11. Jesus predicted not only that he would die, but how he would die. He did this many times (e.g. Matthew 16:21; 17:22-23; 20:17-19; Mark 9:30-32; Luke 18:31-34; John 12:27-28; 13:21).

12. The word 'ransom' is used often in the Bible (e.g. Exodus 30:12; Numbers 35:32; Job 33:24; Psalm 49:5-9). The Bible uses this word to show that someone could pay a ransom and redeem/free a slave (Leviticus 25:47-49), or if someone was condemned to die they could redeem/save their life (Exodus 21:29-30). Sold property could even be redeemed/brought back (Leviticus 25:25-28). God is seen as the redeemer and rescuer because he saved his people from slavery (Exodus 6:6; Deuteronomy 7:8; 9:26; Psalm 74:2; 77:15; Micah 6:4). The word clearly communicates the idea that a ransom price can be paid to redeem/free someone or something. See Holmes, S.R., *The Wondrous Cross*, 23-25, 34-35. See also Hubbard Jr., R.L., 'Redemption', in Alexander, T.D., and Rosner, B.S. (eds.), *New Dictionary of Biblical Theology*, 716-720, esp. 716. See also Morris, L., 'Redemption', in Hawthorne, G.F., Martin, R.P., and Reid, D.G. (eds.), *Dictionary of Paul and His Letters*, 784-786, esp. 784-786.

13. Jesus' death was a ransom, which means the believer is freed and also given a new status. Titus 2:14 says, '[Jesus] gave himself for us to redeem us from all wickedness and to purify for himself a people that are his very own, eager to do what is good.' Robert Hubbard Jr., the seasoned Professor of Biblical Literature, says this teaches us that 'the ransom freed believers from their sins and its penalty'. Timothy Keller, the founder and leader of the Redeemer Presbyterian Church in Manhattan, agrees that this shows Jesus took the sinners place and died instead of them. However, he stresses that the believer also gains a new identity, is adopted into God's family and becomes 'his very own'. This acceptance is a gift from God, given freely through faith, and isn't given based on performance or anything we've done (Philippians 3:8-9). See Hubbard Jr., R.L., 'Redemption', in Alexander, T.D., and Rosner, B.S. (eds.), *New Dictionary of Biblical Theology*, 716-720, esp. 719. See also Keller, T., *Making Sense of God: An Invitation to the Sceptical*, 136-137.

14. The resurrection shows us that Jesus wasn't just a failed revolutionist or criminal who was sentenced to death. He wasn't just someone making false claims or a false messiah either. The resurrection confirms Jesus' true significance because it means he came back to life. This proves he defeated death and overcame sin once and for all, and his way leads to life. The resurrection proves what he said is true and can be trusted. See Tomlin, G., *The Widening Circle: Priesthood as God's Way of Blessing the World*, 40-41.

15. I think it's truly amazing that when Jesus said to his disciples that one of them would betray him, none of them said, 'Well, it's obviously Judas Iscariot. Jesus has always treated him differently and told us not to accept him. He's never been part of the group.' All of the disciples were clueless. They didn't know who Jesus was talking about. I think this suggests that Jesus treated Judas like the other disciples, like a friend, like everyone else, despite knowing what he would do. What an amazing act of love and grace, which would have no doubt made it even more difficult for Jesus to see Judas betray him (John 13:21-30).

16. At the time of Jesus' death, men were normally crucified naked to add to their humiliation. Due to Jewish sensitivities around nakedness, Jesus may have had a loincloth tied around his waist, but he was most likely naked. This would explain why in Luke 23:34 the Roman soldiers divided up his clothes. See Edwards, J.R., *The Gospel According to Luke*, The Pillar New Testament Commentary, Nottingham: Apollos, 2015, 685. See also Carroll, J.T., *Luke: A Commentary*, The New Testament Library, Louisville, KY: Westminster John Knox Press, 2012, 466.

17. In the Old Testament, it says that anyone who is hung on a tree is cursed by God (Deuteronomy 21:23). This type of death was used to punish magical practices and blasphemy, meaning most Jews would have looked down on Jesus because of the way he died. The Romans saw crucifixion as a slave's punishment, reserved for the lower classes, the worst criminals, and enemies of the empire (Luke 23:32-33). They thought this type of death was degrading and painful. In fact, in the first few centuries, the cross was used by non-Christians to mock Christians. They used it to symbolise the foolishness of worshipping a criminal. Some even drew a man with an ass' head dying on the cross to insult Jesus and the Christian faith. See Dennis, J., 'Death of Jesus', in Green, J.B., Brown, J.K., and Perrin, N. (eds.), *Dictionary of Jesus and the Gospels*, Second Edition, Nottingham: IVP, 2013, 172-193, esp. 177. See also Whittock, M., and Whittock, E., *Christ: The First 2000 Years*, 149. See also Wilson, B.R., 'The Crucifixion Scene as the Climax of Lukan Inclusively', *Expository Times* 127 (June 2016), 430-438, 437.

18. Crucifixion was a particularly painful death. Nails through the arm and feet would hold the person in place and death would come through blood

loss or asphyxiation after hours, or even days, of suffering. This is partly why Jesus is seen as the 'Suffering Servant' spoken about in Isaiah 50 and 53. See Beers, H., 'Servant of Yahweh', in Green, J.B., Brown, J.K., and Perrin, N. (eds.), *Dictionary of Jesus and the Gospels,* Second Edition, 855-859, esp. 856-7. See also Dennis, J., 'Death of Jesus', in Green, J. B., Brown, J. K., and Perrin, N. (eds.), *Dictionary of Jesus and the Gospels,* Second Edition, 172-193, esp. 173-174. See also Holmes, S.R., *The Wondrous Cross*, 23-25, 34-35.

Chapter 3
'Does my life matter?'
Christ imparts purpose

1. The Bible paints a picture of God creating a new heaven and new earth at the end of time, where sin will no longer exist, God will live and be present with the believers, have close fellowship with them, and bless them. 2 Peter 3:13 says, 'But in keeping with his promise we are looking forward to a new heaven and a new earth, where righteousness dwells.' (See also Isaiah 65:17; 66:22; Revelation 21:1-2,6-7,10-11.) However, we must remember that the Bible says this place, this kingdom, will be established on *this* earth, and God will live with his people on *this* earth. Not in some other 'spiritual realm'. Which is why Jesus teaches his followers to pray 'your kingdom come . . . on earth as it is in heaven' (Matthew 6:10). See Grudem, W., *Systematic Theology: An Introduction to Biblical Doctrine*, 1158-1164. See also Wright, N.T., 'Imagining the Kingdom: Mission and Theology in Early Christianity', *Scottish Journal of Theology* 65 (2012) 379-401, esp. 383, 396. See also endnote 2 from this chapter.

2. The kingdom of God, which is also referred to as the kingdom of heaven, appears frequently in the teachings of Jesus (e.g. Matthew 3:2; 4:17; Mark 1:15; Luke 11:20). Many books have been written on this subject, but to summarise without trying to simplify: the kingdom of God is the place where God dwells (e.g. Psalm 115:2-3) and his rule is fully followed. At the end of time God will fully establish his kingdom on Earth. This

means he will live among his believers, and we will totally follow his rule, meaning their will be no more sin, pain, or suffering (Revelation 21:2-4). Believers will experience fully loving connected relationships free from disconnection. However, this kingdom isn't just a future reality (1 Thessalonians 2:12; 2 Thessalonians 1:5) because Jesus has started to build the kingdom of God on this earth already. Tom Wright, a leading British New Testament scholar, emphasises that the Gospels show that through Jesus, God is becoming King of this world and bringing his kingdom down to Earth. Jesus can achieve this because he is God and came down to Earth (John 1:14; 2:21), and he died and was resurrected. Therefore, the kingdom of God has started to be built on Earth already. Furthermore, believers are told to keep building his kingdom, which we do when we change our lifestyle, character and decisions, with the help of his Spirit, so that through us God reshapes the world around Jesus' life, teaching, death and resurrection. Believers get to experience and be used to (partly) build the kingdom, the new reality which is free from sin and disconnection, in the present. The Bible makes this clear, for example, in the parables of the hidden treasure and the pearl, where the purchaser takes possession immediately (Matthew 13:44-46). The follower of God gives up everything for the kingdom but receives it, and receives new life, there and then. (See also John 5:24; 6:53-55; Luke 10:25,28.) The kingdom of God is therefore God's active rule, presence and intervention in history and the present age. It's active and dynamic, but also a state of peace, happiness and blessing, which can be experienced by those who enter in. The Church and the community of Christians is the main expression of God's kingdom on Earth because this is where we have fellowship, are unified to Jesus and live under his rule whilst loving him and others. But God's kingdom also reaches beyond the Church. Wherever Christians choose to love their neighbour because of their relationship to Jesus, the kingdom is made visible and becomes a present reality. Believers are used by God to build his kingdom and lay the foundations, by building loving connections with God and others, in the way Jesus did. See France, R.T., *The New International Commentary on the New Testament: The Gospel of Matthew*, Grand Rapids, MI: Eerdmans, 2007, 540. See also Kreitzer, L.J., 'Kingdom of God/Christ', in Hawthorne, G.F., Martin, R.P., and Reid, D.G. (eds.), *Dictionary of Paul and His Letters*, 524-526, esp. 524. See also Maston, J., 'How Wrong were the Disciples about the Kingdom? Thoughts on Acts 1:6', *Expository*

Times 126 (January 2015) 169-178, esp. 171-173, 176. See also Osborne, G.R., 'Life, Eternal Life', in Green, J.B., Brown, J.K., and Perrin, N. (eds.), *Dictionary of Jesus and the Gospels,* Second Edition, 518-522, esp. 521. See also Walton, S., 'The Kingdom of God and the Church', *Churchman* 129 (Winter 2015) 305-317, esp. 308, 309, 312, 317. See also Welby, J., *Dethroning Mammon: Making Money Serve Grace*, London: Bloomsbury, 2016, 1-7, 77-78, 94-97. See also Wright, N.T., 'Imagining the Kingdom: Mission and Theology in Early Christianity', *Scottish Journal of Theology* 65 (2012) 379-401, esp. 382-383, 386-387, 396, 398-399, 401.

3. An eighty-year-long Harvard study that followed, and is still following, more than 1,000 people during the course of their lives, found that strong relationships seems to be the most vital criteria for a long and happy life. See Mineo, L., 'Good Genes Are Nice, But Joy Is Better: Harvard study, almost 80 years old, has proved that embracing community helps us live longer, and be happier', *Harvard Gazette* website 11 April 2017, https://news.harvard.edu/gazette/story/2017/04/over-nearly-80-years-harvard-study-has-been-showing-how-to-live-a-healthy-and-happy-life/ (accessed 28.2.18).

4. I always say that no model or picture for understanding the cross and resurrection is perfect. There isn't one model that will be able to explain everything Jesus overcame and restored. For example, the Connection Model doesn't outline the impact Jesus' ministry has on creation. Creation wasn't at peace with God after the Fall, but through Jesus' obedience creation was given peace (Colossians 1:19-20; Hebrews 1:2). This aspect is important, which is why multiple models and pictures, multiple tools in the toolbox, are needed. See endnote 1 from the prologue.

5. Tom Smail, who was a leading Scottish theologian in the charismatic movement, highlights the importance of the triune God existing in loving relationship. He says God is love, and can love people freely because before he created humanity, God the Father in the Spirit was loving God the Son, and the Son was loving the Father in the Spirit – 'He does not need us in order to have an object for his love. He is in his own life both the loving father and the beloved son who fulfil their love for each other in the loving Spirit who mediates and perfects their love. Because God is love in himself, his love for us is not a necessity of his

being, but a free act of grace'. God's nature must be understood as love. See Smail, T., *Like Father, Like Son: The Trinity Imaged in Our Humanity*, 154-156.

6. Believers are reconciled to God through Jesus' death and saved through his life (Romans 5:10), which leads to a new identity and a transformation that allows us to share his love with others. It all starts with God, who is bigger than humanity and our flaws. When we become Christians, we're reconciled and made holy in God's sight, and we're brought into a relationship with God and are forgiven, gain the status of a friend and family member, and are no longer condemned or enemies (Romans 8:1-13; Colossians 1:21-22; Hebrews 10:19-25; 1 John 3:1-3). This new identity and reconciliation with God also leads to true reconciliation with others too, because the same love that connects God the Father and God the Son, connects God to us, and this love then overflows and connects us with others as we pass it on to those around us. See Lane, S.T., and Tripp, P.D., *Relationships: A Mess Worth Making*, esp. 13, 26-27. See also Macleod, D., *Christ Crucified: Understanding the Atonement*, 169-170. See also Duncan, M., *One For All: The Foundations,* Oxford: Monarch Books, 2017, 60.

7. Jesus tells his disciples to pick up their cross in Luke 9:23-26.

8. Persecution is when people are repeatedly and systematically inflicted with serious harm, deprived of human rights, arrested or killed, because of their religion, race, nationality, political beliefs or things that make them different. At start of 2018, it's reported that that at least 3,000 Christians were killed for their faith in the previous year. More than 200 million Christians in the fifty most difficult countries to be a Christian experience very high levels of persecution. These persecution levels are set to rise as governments and other groups try to eradicate Christians and Christianity from their countries. (This information was taken from the following websites in January 2018, and was accurate on this date; these websites will also record the latest information and stories involving persecuted Christians: www. opendoorsuk.org, www.releaseinternational.org, www.barnabasfund. org, www.christianfreedom.org, and www.persecution.com).

9. Anyone can become a Christian and join God's family. In Acts 11:26 it says, 'The disciples were called Christians first at Antioch.' This very important verse could easily be missed, but it comes after a lot of momentum has been building in the book of Acts. In the first few chapters the apostles had been telling the Jews about Jesus, meaning the first followers of Jesus would have all come from a Jewish faith background. Then in Acts 8, the Samaritans hear about Jesus and become followers. Then in Acts 9 Paul meets with Jesus and believes in him. God himself then says he will send Paul to the Gentiles, those who aren't part of the Jewish faith, with the message of Jesus (Acts 9:15). Then in Acts 10 Peter is shown in a vision from God and the Gentile Cornelius, his friends and relatives, received the Holy Spirit and become followers of Jesus (Acts 10:1-23,44-48). In Acts 11:1-18 the Jews who believed in Jesus and the apostles eventually agree that the Gentiles are allowed to follow Jesus without becoming Jewish first. Then in Act 11:19-24 more believers begin to preach to the Gentiles as well. We then arrive at Acts 11:26, which says that for the first time, the followers of Jesus are called Christians. This is so important because it shows us that being a Christian is no longer about following Jewish customs, coming from the right background, what you did or believed before, or anything other than accepting God's unconditional love and Jesus as our Saviour. God's new family has no barriers (Matthew 12:46-50).

10. Donald Macleod, the retired professor and principal, argues that reconciliation with God is humanity's greatest need, and this truth needs to be urgently shared and preached. That's why Christians get given a ministry of reconciliation (2 Corinthians 5:19). Believers need to tell people who feel alienated, unwelcome, and absent, that there is peace and connection with God through the cross and resurrection. See Macleod, D., *Christ Crucified: Understanding the Atonement*, 157.

11. John 17:3 stresses that 'eternal life' isn't mainly about living forever and being resurrected after death (even though this aspect is true and important), but about knowing, encountering and relating to God. This idea is taught in the rest of John, and the New Testament too, which shows that 'eternal life' is mainly about having a life that reflects 'the age to come'. This 'age to come' is the place where there is no sin or separation between God and us, and where his purposes are unhindered. 'The age

to come' will be fully established and experienced at the end of time when God creates a new heaven and a new earth, but this future reality invades the present reality and believers experience 'the age to come' now. This is because we have crossed form 'death' to 'life' already because of Jesus (John 5:24; John 6:54). In addition, the word 'know' in John 17:3 is about more than just intellectual knowledge, it communicates the idea of having communion, fellowship and relationship. This emphasises that 'eternal life' is about having a relationship and closeness with God primarily. Those of us living in 'eternal life' get to immediately experience a connected relationship with God and others, which will continue after we die because God had defeated death (Romans 6:23; 1 Corinthians 15:20-28; Daniel 12:2), and will bring us back to life and restore the relationship, and we will then live forever with him. So 'eternal life' does have an eternal aspect to it, but it's mainly about experiencing a relationship with the eternal God, now and in the future. (See 1 Thessalonians 4:13-18; Revelation 6:9-11; 15:2.) See Beasley-Murray, G.R., Word Biblical Commentary, Volume 36, *John,* Second Edition, Nashville, TN: Thomas Nelson, 1999, 297. See also Johnson, D.H., 'Life', in Alexander, T.D., and Rosner, B.S. (eds.), *New Dictionary of Biblical Theology,* Leicester: IVP, 2006, 640-644, esp. 643-644. See also Osborne, G.R., 'Life, Eternal Life', in Green, J.B., Brown, J.K., and Perrin, N. (eds.), *Dictionary of Jesus and the Gospels,* Second Edition, 518-522, esp. 520-521. See also Williams, R., *God With Us: The Meaning of the Cross and Resurrection. Then and Now*, 90. See also endnote 9 from chapter 1.

12. There are examples in the Bible where God speaks to people in dreams and/or vision, and they aren't only given to Christians (e.g. Matthew 27:19; Acts 10:1-8,24,44-48). God also directly speaks to people. Like in arguably the most famous example, when he speaks to Saul, who is also called Paul, on the road to Damascus (Acts 9:1-22).

13. The traditional Christian view teaches that God will one day judge everyone after we die. Those who put their faith in Jesus will be saved, and those who do not will be punished by being tortured forever. However, some Christians have questioned what this 'punishment' actually refers to. On the whole, most Christian denominations think this punishment does mean that unbelievers will suffer ongoing eternal

torture (e.g. Revelation 20:10,15; Mark 9:47-48, Luke 16:23-25). However, the idea that punishment could mean unbelievers are destroyed, and no longer exist instead of being tortured forever, is upheld by some Christians (e.g. Matthew 10:28; 7:13; 1 Timothy 6:9). Either way, the Bible is clear that non-believers are judged and separated from God and his kingdom after the final judgement. See Boyd, G.A., and Eddy, P.R., *Across the Spectrum: Understanding Issues in Evangelical Theology*, Grand Rapids, MI: Baker, 2005, 254-264.

To continue the discussion, go to:

www.samecrossnewquestions.com

Or follow me:

 Same Cross New Questions

@AndreAdefope

andreadefope

You may also be interested in:

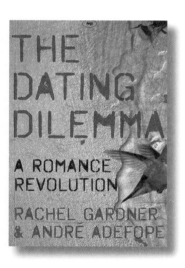

Rachel Gardner and André Adefope look at God's guidelines for romance. They ask the difficult questions, but they also ask how God helps us to change – how you can become a godly boyfriend: confident in who you are, supportive, worthy of respect; or a godly girlfriend: sure of yourself, able to nurture selflessness and generosity in relationships.